Benoni Lanctot

Chinese and English phrase book : with the Chinese pronunciation indicated in English

Specially adapted for the use of merchants, travelers and families. Second Edition

Benoni Lanctot

Chinese and English phrase book : with the Chinese pronunciation indicated in English

Specially adapted for the use of merchants, travelers and families. Second Edition

ISBN/EAN: 9783337208233

Printed in Europe, USA, Canada, Australia, Japan

Cover: Foto ©Paul-Georg Meister /pixelio.de

More available books at **www.hansebooks.com**

語通英華

CHINESE AND ENGLISH
PHRASE BOOK,

WITH THE CHINESE PRONUNCIATION
INDICATED IN ENGLISH,

SPECIALLY ADAPTED FOR THE USE OF

MERCHANTS, TRAVELERS AND FAMILIES.

BY

BENONI LANCTOT.

SECOND EDITION, REVISED AND ENLARGED.

San Francisco:
A. ROMAN & COMPANY,
BOOKSELLERS, PUBLISHERS AND IMPORTERS,
417 AND 419 MONTGOMERY STREET.
NEW YORK: 17 MERCER STREET.

1867.

Entered according to Act of Congress, in the year 1867, by

B. LANCTOT,

In the Clerk's Office of the District Court of the United States, in and for the Northern District of California.

PREFACE.

The object of the author in publishing this little volume, is to enable all classes of citizens to acquire an elementary and practical knowledge of the spoken language of the Cantonese dialect.

This is the dialect most generally understood by all classes of Chinese immigrants on the Pacific coast and elsewhere, as nearly all such immigrants are from the Canton district; the comparatively few who come from other districts soon become, through a necessary and continual intercourse with the Cantonese, familiarized with the accent and pronunciation of the latter. So that a man well versed in this dialect may be readily understood by all the Chinese; as the Chinese almost without exception read their language, the indication of the proper sentence will readily be understood by them.

It will also be found sufficient in communicating with the merchants and educated classes of Japan, as they understand the Chinese characters.

The author has been induced to undertake this publication by what seemed to him a daily increasing necessity, consequent upon the extended employment of Chinese, and the now established regular line of communication with China and Japan.

The work is adapted to practical use in business and social life, and as such is respectfully submitted to the public.

THE AUTHOR.

San Francisco, February 25th, 1867.

CONTENTS.

	Page.
About income tax	67
Articles of food	16
Bedroom	77
Breakfast	31
Business conversation	39
Crockery	74
Cutlery	75
Days and months	9
Dialogue on getting a China boy	21
Dinner	35
Dress	75
Dressing-room	78
Earthenware	74
Evening orders	24
Familiar sentences	30
Fruit	13
Glassware	75
Grain	14
House furniture	72
Liquors	19
Lunch	35
Names of colors	12
Numerals	10
On meeting a friend	44
Porcelain	74
Quadrupeds	79
School, the	45
Short sentences	49
Spirits	19
Tea	39
Teas	19
Traveler's conversation	41
Verbs	81
Vocabulary of useful words	72

RULES FOR PRONUNCIATION.

(´) The acute denotes the rising inflection.
(`) The grave denotes the falling inflection.
Each Chinese character corresponds to the Chinese word above it, in English letters.
a as in *pan*.
aa as in *fawn*.
e as in *they*.
i as in *machine*.
o final, as in *go*.
oh as in *horn*.
oo as in *food*.
ue as in *oeil* (French.)
ai as *y* in *fly*.
au as *ow* in *how*.
eu as in *peu* (French.)
iu as *ee* with *ou* in *see-you*.
oi as *oy* in *boy*.
ooi as in *cooing*.
sz a buzzing sound.
m as the elementary sound in the English letter.
ng as *n* in *no*.
ngo a protracted full nasal sound of *no*.
h in the words *shap, shat, sheung*, etc., is soft.

THE VERB.—*Moods* and *tenses*, as such, are quite unknown to the Chinese. No distinction is made between *active* and *passive* verbs; nor are the *persons* or *numbers* noticed at all by them. The context and the circumstances under which any thing is said are the chief guides to the exact sense of any passage. *Time* and *mode* are very clearly shown by the meaning of the whole sentence, or by the conditions under which it has been uttered.

"To-morrow I shall go" would be expressed in Chinese by "to-morrow I go;" "yesterday I came" would be expressed by "yesterday I come."

CHINESE AND ENGLISH PHRASE BOOK.

DAYS AND MONTHS.

Sunday.	Monday.	Tuesday.	Wednesday.
Lai′ paai` yat.	Lai′ paai` yat.	Lat paai i.	Lai` paai′ saam`.
禮拜日	禮拜一	禮拜二	禮拜三

Thursday.	Friday.	Saturday.
Lai′ paai` sze`.	Lai′ paai` ng′.	Lai′ paai` luk.
禮拜四	禮拜五	禮拜六

One week.
Yat koh` lai′ paai`.
一個禮拜

January.	February.	March.	April.
Ying ching uet.	I` uet.	Saam uet.	Sze` uet.
英正月	二月	三月	四月
May.	June.	July.	August.
Ng′ uet.	Luk uet.	Tsat uet.	Paat uet.
五月	六月	七月	八月
September.	October.	November.	December.
Kau′ uet.	Shap uet.	Shap yat uet.	Shap i` uet.
九月	十月	十一月	十二月

One year.
Yat nin.

一年.

1 One.	2 Two.	3 Three.	4 Four.	5 Five.
Yat.	*i.*	*Sam.*	*Si.*	*Ng.*

一丨. 二刂. 三川. 四人. 五𠄌.

6 Six.	7 Seven.	8 Eight.	9 Nine.	10 Ten.
Lok.	*Tsat.*	*Pat.*	*Kou.*	*Shap.*

六上. 七𠄎. 八三. 九攵. 十卄.

11 Eleven.	12 Twelve.	13 Thirteen.	14 Fourteen.
Shap yat.	*Shap i.*	*Shap sam.*	*Shap si.*

十一卜. 十二𠆢. 十三三. 十四以

15 Fifteen.	16 Sixteen.	17 Seventeen.	18 Eighteen.
Shap ng.	*Shap lok.*	*Shap tsat.*	*Shap pat.*

十五𠄎. 十六凵. 十七𠆢. 十八日

19 Nineteen.	20 Twenty.	21 Twenty-one.	30 Thirty.
Shap kou.	*i shap.*	*i shap yat.*	*Sam shap.*

十九攵. 二十卄. 二十一卜. 三十卄.

40 Forty.	50 Fifty.	60 Sixty.	70 Seventy.	80 Eighty.
Si shap.	*Ng shap.*	*Lok shap.*	*Tsat shap.*	*Pat shap.*

四十卄. 五十卅. 六十卄. 七十卄. 八十三

90 Ninety.	100 One hundred.	200 Two hundred.
Kou shap.	*Yat pak.*	*i pak.*

九十卄. 一伯佰. 二伯佰.

500 Five hundred.	1000 One thousand.
Ng pak.	*Yat tsin.*

五伯佰. 一仟仟.

2000 Two thousand.	5000 Five thousand.
i tsin.	*Ng tsin.*

二仟仟. 伍仟仟.

NUMERALS.

10,000 Ten thousand.
Yat man'.
一萬丙.

1,000,000 One million.
Yat pak man'.
一伯萬另.

1867 Eighteen hundred and sixty-seven.
Yat tsin pat pak lok shap tsat.
一仟八伯六十七 .

San Francisco, January 21st, 1867.
Tai fau ching ut i shap yat ho, yat tsin pat pak lok shap tsat nin.
大埠正月二十一號一仟八伯六十七年

First.	Second.	Third.	Fourth.	Fifth.	Sixth.
Tai yat.	Tai i.	Tai sam.	Tai sz̄.	Tai ng.	Tai lok.
第一.	第二.	第三.	第四.	第五.	第六

Seventh.	Eighth.	Ninth.	Tenth.	Eleventh.
Tai tsat.	Tai pat.	Tai kau.	Tai shap.	Tai shap yat.
第七.	第八.	第九.	第十.	第十一

Twelfth.	Thirteenth.	Fourteenth.	Fifteenth.
Tai shap i.	Tai shap sam.	Tai shap sz̄.	Tai shap ng.
第十二.	第十三.	第十四.	第十四.

Sixteenth.	Seventeenth.	Eighteenth.	Nineteenth.
Tai shap lok.	Tai shap tsat.	Tai shap pat.	Tai shap kau
第十六.	第十七.	第十八.	第十九.

Twentieth.	Twenty-first.	Thirtieth.
Tai i shap.	Tai i shap yat.	Tai sam shap.
第二十.	第二十一.	第三十.

Fortieth.	Fiftieth.	Sixtieth.	Seventieth.
Tai sz̄ shap.	Tai ng shap.	Tai lok shap.	Tai tsat shap.
第四十.	第五十.	第六十.	第七十.

Eightieth.	Ninetieth.	Hundredth.
Tai pat shap	Tai kau shap.	Tai yat pak.
第八十.	第九十.	第一伯.

NUMERALS.

One-half.	One-third.	One-quarter.
Yat poon.	Sam fan yat.	Sz fan yat.
一半.	三份一.	四份一

One-fifth.	One-eighth.	One-tenth.	One pair.
Ng fan yat.	Pat fan yat.	Shap fan yat.	Yat tooi.
五份一.	八份一.	十份一.	一對.

One dozen.	One score.	One gross.
Shap i koh.	i shap koh.	Shap i koh ta sun.
十二個.	二十個.	十二個打臣

Once.	Twice.	Thrice.	Four times.
Yat chu.	i chu.	Sam chu.	Si chu.
一次.	二次.	三次.	四次.

One fold.	Two fold.	Ten fold.	One hundred fold.
Yat pooi.	i pooi.	Shap pooi.	Yat pak pooi.
一倍.	二倍.	十倍.	一伯倍.

One bag.	One bale.	One basket.	One bit.	One bottle.
Yat pau.	Yat kwan.	Yat loh.	Yat tik.	Yat tsun.
一包.	一綑.	一籮.	一錨.	一的.

One box.	One bundle.	One cask.	One cart-full.	One fan.
Yat seung.	Yat chaut.	Yat tung tsai.	Yat che'.	Yat fan.
一箱.	一扎.	一桶仔.	一車.	一分.

One foot.	One glass.	One inch.	One invoice of goods.	One jar.
Yat chek.	Yat pooi.	Yat tsuen`.	Yat taan` foh`.	Yat ching.
一尺.	一杯.	一寸.	一單貨.	一埕.

One line.	One package.	One pair.	One pane of glass.	One piece.
Yat hang.	Yat sin poo'.	Yat tooi.	Yat fai poh li.	Yat kin.
一行.	一小包.	一對.	一塊玻璃.	一件.

One piece of cloth.	One sheet of paper.	One set.	One spoonful.
Yat pat poo'.	Yat cheung chi'.	Yat foo'.	Yat king.
一疋布.	一張紙.	一副.	一羹.

FRUIT.

FRUIT.
Kwoh 'tsze
果子.

Acorn.	Almonds.	Apple.	Apricot.
Heuen tsz.	*Hang yan.*	*Ping kwoh'.*	*Wong mooi.*
橡子.	杏仁.	苹菓.	黄梅.

Chestnut.	Citron.	Cocoanuts.	Dates.
Fung lut.	*Fut shau'.*	*Ye' tsz.*	*Pak tso'.*
風栗.	佛手.	椰子.	白棗.

Red Dates.	Fig.	Grape.	Groundnut.
Hung tso'.	*Mo' fa' kwoh*	*Poo tai tsz.*	*Fa' shang.*
紅棗.	無花果.	葡提子.	花生

Lemon,—Lime.		Olive.	Sour Orange.
Ning mung.		*Kom lam'.*	*Tim chang'.*
檸檬.		橄欖.	甜橙.

Peach.		Pear.	Pine Apple.
To'		*Sha' li.*	*Poh loh.*
桃.		沙梨.	波蘿.

Plantain.	Plum.	Red Plum.	Sour Plum.
Tsiu.	*Mooi.*	*Hung mooi.*	*Suen mooi.*
蕉.	梅.	紅梅.	酸梅.

Pomegranate.	Prunes.	Quince.	Raisins.
Shek laue.	*Ying tsz.*	*Man sau kwoh'*	*Potai tsz.*
石榴.	櫻子.	萬壽果.	葡提子.

	Strawberry.		Walnuts.
	Yeung mooi.		*Hat to'.*
	楊梅.		核桃.

GRAIN.—VEGETABLES.

GRAIN.		VEGETABLES.	
Ng kuk loi.		Kwa' tsoi loi.	
五谷類.		疏菜類.	
Barley.	Buckwheat.	Corn.	Maize.
Tai muk.	Sam kok mak.	Woh.	Suk mai.
大麥.	三角麥.	禾.	粟米.
Millet.	Pearl barley.	Rice.	Red rice.
Suk.	Yi mai.	Mai.	Hung mai.
粟.	苡米.	米.	紅米.
White rice.	Sago.	Wheat.	Oats.
Pak mai.	Sai mai.	Mak.	Cheung mak.
白米.	西米.	麥.	長麥.
Bean.	Long-bean.		Soy-bean.
Tsam tau`.	Tau` kok.		Pak tau`.
蠶豆.	豆角.		白豆.
Red beans.	Black beans.		Cabbage.
Hung tau`.	Hak tau`.		Ye' tsoi.
紅豆.	黑豆.		椰菜.
Carrot.	Cauliflower.		Cayenne pepper.
Hung loh pa`k.	Fa' ye' tsoi.		Lat tsiu.
紅蘿蔔.	花椰菜.		辣椒.
Celery.	Cress.	Cucumber.	Egg plant.
Tong ho`.	Shui kan.	Wong kwa'.	Foo' kwa'.
塘蒿.	水芹.	黄瓜.	苦瓜.
Garlic.	Ginger.	Squash.	Greens.
Tsing' suen.	Ke'ung.	Kwa'.	Tsing' tsoi.
青蒜.	羗.	瓠.	青菜.
Watergreens.		Wintergreens.	
Ang tsoi.		Tsu na' tsoi.	
蕹菜.		猪姆菜.	

VEGETABLES.

Lettuce.	Melon.	Mushroom.
Shang tsoi'.	*Kwa'.*	*Heung sun.*
生菜	瓜	香信

Muskmelon.	Mustard.	Onion.
Heun'g kwa'.	*Kai tsoi.*	*Tsung tau.*
香瓜	芥菜	葱頭

Parsley.	Peas.	Green peas.	Black pepper.
Hon kan tsoi.	*Ho lan tau.*	*Luk tau.*	*Hoo tsiu.*
旱芹菜	荷蘭豆	綠豆	胡椒

Potato.	Sweet potato.	Pumpkin.
Ho lan shu.	*Fan shu.*	*Tung kwa'.*
荷蘭薯	番薯	冬瓜

Sugar cane.	Tomato.	Turnip.
Che'.	*Fan ke'.*	*Lo' pak.*
蔗	番茄	蘿蔔

Watermelon.	Yam.
Sai kwa'.	*Tai shu.*
西瓜	大薯

Chinese pepper.	Yellow pumpkin.	Purslane.
Chun tsiu.	*Naam' kwa'.*	*Chu tsai tsoi.*
川椒	南瓜	猪仔菜

Scallions.	Sea-weed.	Edible sea-weed.	Sesamum.
Kau tsoi.	*Hoi' tsoi'.*	*Tsz tsoi'.*	*Chi ma.*
韭菜	海菜	紫菜	芝蔴

Sow-thistle.	Spinage.	Taro.	Water-chestnut.
Foo tsoi'.	*Hin tsoi'.*	*Oo tau.*	*Ma' tai.*
苦菜	莧菜	芋頭	馬蹄

Water caltrops.	Water-lily seeds.	Water-lily roots.
Ling kok.	*Lin tsz.*	*Lin ngau.*
菱角	蓮子	蓮藕

ARTICLES OF FOOD.
Shik mat.
食物.

English	Romanization	Chinese
Anchovy.	Tso'u kai.	槽魚䱥.
Dried apples.	Ping kwoh kon.	平菓乾.
Bacon.	Yin yuk.	烟肉.
Beans.	Tau kok.	荳角.
Batter.	Min liu.	麵料.
Beef.	Ngau yuk.	牛肉.
Boiled beef.	Shap ngau yuk.	烚牛肉.
Roast beef.	Shiu ngau yuk.	燒牛肉.
Salt beef.	Ham ngau yuk.	咸牛肉.
Beef steak.	Tit pa' ngau yuk.	鉄耙牛肉.
Birds.	Tse'uk tsai.	雀仔.
Biscuit.	Min ping' con.	麵餅干.
Bread.	Min' tau.	麵頭.
Bran bread.	Mak hong min tau.	麥糠麵頭.
Bran.	Mak hong.	麥糠.
Broth.	Tong.	湯.
Butter.	Ngau yau.	牛油.
Cabbage.	Ye' tsoi.	椰菜.
Cake.	Peng'.	餅.
Wine cake.	Tsau peng.'	酒餅.
Capon.	Sin kai.	剗雞.
Cheese.	Ngau nai peng'.	牛奶餅.
Chicken.	Kai hong.	鷄項.
Chocolate.	Chu ko la't.	猪古辛.
Chowder.	U kang.	魚羹.
Coffee.	Ka' fe'.	喀啡.
Cream.	Ngau yu yau.	牛乳油.
Crab soup.	Hai yuk tong.	蟹肉湯.
Curry.	Wong ke'aony.	黄羗.
Curry beef.	Ka li ngau yuk.	喀利牛肉.
Custards.	Kat shi.	吉時.
Cutlets.	Kat lit.	吉烈.
Duck.	Ap'.	鴨.
Roast duck.	Shiu ap'.	燒鴨.
Dough.	Tiu min.	調麵.
Egg.	Kai tan.	鷄旦.
Cow's feet.	Ngau keuk.	牛脚.
Fillet of pork.	Chu pi cham.	猪肶砧.
Fish.	U.	魚.

ARTICLES OF FOOD.

Fresh fish.	Salt fish.	Boiled fish.
Sin u.	Ham` u.	Pak shap u.
鮮魚	咸魚	白烚魚

Fried fish.	Flour.	Fowl.	Roasted fowl.
Chau u.	Min fun.	Kai.	Shiu kai.
煠魚	麵粉	雞	燒雞

Fricasseed fowl.	Goose.		Roasted Goose.
Fat lan sai kai.	ngoh.		Shiu ngoh.
佛嚹西雞	鵞		燒鵞

Gravy.	Rice gruel.	Ham.	Hash.
Chup.	Mai hu'.	Fo'h' tooi	Hat shik.
汁	米糊	火腿	吃食

Mutton.	Sheep's head.	Honey.	Preserve.
Ye ung yuk.	Yeung shau.	Mat tong.	Tong ko`.
羊肉	羊首	蜜糖	糖膏

Pig's foot jelly.	Jellies.		Lard.
Chue keuk tu'ng.	Che' li.		Chue yau.
猪腳凍	車厘		猪油

Maize.	Indian meal.	Milk.	Goat's milk.
Suk.	Suk mai.	Ngau ue'.	Yeung ue'.
粟	粟米	牛乳	羊乳

Molasses.	Mustard.	Nutmeg.	Sweet oil.
Kut shui tong.	Kai moot.	Tau` kau`.	Sang tsoi yau.
桔水糖	芥末	荳蔻	生菜油

Oyster.	Liver of beef.		Liver of pork.
Ho	Ngau kohn		Chue kohn.
蠔	牛肝		猪肝

Pancakes.	Partridge.	Pastry.	Pig.	Baked pig.
Pan kik.	Che` koo.	Min shik.	Chuu tsai.	Kuk chue tsai.
班戟	鷓鴣	麵食	猪仔	焗猪仔

ARTICLES OF FOOD.

Pig's feet.	Pickles.	Pigeon.	Pork chops.
Chue keuk.	Suen kwoh.	Pak kop.	Chue pai kwat.
猪脚	酸菓	白鴿	猪排骨

Salt pork.	Roasted pork.		Baked potatoes.
Ham chue yuk.	Shiu yuk.		Kuk shue tsai.
咸猪肉	燒肉		局薯仔

Sweet potatoes.	Pudding.	Bread pudding.	Rabbit.
Hung shue.	Poo tin.	Min tau poo tin.	To tsai.
紅薯	布顛	麵頭布顛	兔仔

Rice pudding.	Rice.	Salt.	Sausages.	Snipes.
Faan poo tin.	Faan.	im.	Yeong cheung.	Sa chui.
飯布顛	飯	鹽	釀腸	沙椎

Soup.	Beef soup.	Mutton soup.	Fowl soup.
Tong.	Ngau yuk tong.	Yeung yuk tong.	Kai tong.
湯	牛肉湯	羊肉湯	雞湯

Turtle.	Turtle soup.	Spare rib.	Soy.	Sugar.
Shui yu.	Shui yu tong.	Chu mi lung.	Shi yau.	Tong.
水魚	水魚湯	猪尾龍	豉油	糖

Beef suet.	Sweet meats.	Tart.	Plum tart.
Ngau kwat sui.	Tong kwoh.	Tu't.	Mooi ta't.
牛骨髓	糖菓	噠	梅噠

Toast.	Turkey.		Roasted turkey.
To se.	Foh kai.		Shiu foh kai.
哆嗉	火鷄		燒火鷄

Veal.	Vermicelli.	Vinegar.	Yam.	Yeast.
Ngau tsai yuk.	Fun sze.	Tso.	Tai shu.	Kau.
牛仔肉	粉絲	醋	大薯	酵

Yolk.		Cold meat.	Victuals.
Tan wong.		Tung yuk.	Foh sik.
蛋黃		凍肉	火食

SPIRITS.—LIQUORS.—TEAS.

Spirits—Liquors.	Wine.	Arrack.	Beer.
Tsau'.	Win tsau'.	A' lik tsau'.	Pe' tsau.
酒	呍酒	啞力酒	啤酒
Champagne.	Cider.	Claret.	Gin.	Madeira.
Sam pin' tsau'.	Ping kwo' tsau'.	Hung tsau'.	Tsin tsau'.	I ik tsau'.
三边酒	平菓酒	紅酒	煎酒	白酒
Port Wine.	Porter.	Brandy.	Cherry Cordial.
Poot tsau'.	Po ta' tsau'.	Pa' lan' te.	Che' le pa' lan' te.
砵酒	波打酒	罷蘭地	車厘罷蘭地
Sherry.	Rum.	Old Tom.	Soda Water.
Che' li tsau'.	Lum tsau'.	O'-lo tom.	So ta' shui.
車厘酒	啉酒	澳魯泵	梳打水
Lemonade.		Lemon syrup.
Ning mong shui.		Ning mong tong.
檸檬水		檸檬糖
Tea.	Pecco.	Orange Pecco.	Inferior Pecco
Cha.	Pa'k ho.	Seung heung.	Chu ho'.
茶	白毫	上香	紫毫
Hung Muy.	Black Tea.	Congo.	Fine Congo.
Hung mooi.	Hung cha.	Kung foo cha.	Nuen chong kung foo cha
紅梅	紅茶	工夫茶	嫩裝工夫茶
Common Congo.	Souchong.	Powchong.
Tso' kung foo cha'.	Shiu chung.	Pau chong.
粗工夫茶	小種	色種
Oolung.	Green Tea.	Gunpowder.	No. 1 Gunpowder.
Oo lung.	Luk cha.	Chu cha.	Ha' muk.
烏龍	綠茶	珠茶	蝦目
Imperial.	Hyson.	Common Hyson.
Oon chu.	Hi chun.	Foo hi.
元珠	熙春	付熙

TEAS.

No. 1 Young Hyson.	Old Hyson.	Chulan.	Sunglo.
Ngo mi.	*Hi pi.*	*Chu la'n.*	*Chunglo.*
娥眉	熙皮	珠蘭	松蘿

Campoi.		Caper Congo.		Scented Tea.
Kan poi.		*Chung chai.*		*Fa' he'ung.*
揀焙		松制		花香

TASTE.	Tasteless.	Salt.	Sour.	Sweet.	Bitter.
Mi.	*Mo mi.*	*Ha'm.*	*Suen.*	*Tim.*	*Foo'.*
味	無味	咸	酸	甜	苦

Hot.	Fragrant.	Bad smell.		Strong.	Weak.
La't.	*Heung.*	*Chau.*		*Nung.*	*Tam.*
辣	香	臭		濃	淡

Cold.	Hot.	Cool.	Dry.	Wet.	Oily.	Lean.
Lang'.	*it.*	*Leung.*	*Kohn.*	*Shup.*	*Fi.*	*Shau.*
冷	熱	涼	乾	濕	肥	瘦

NAMES OF COLOURS.—Black.	Blue-black.	Blue.	Azure-blue.
Hak shik.	*Lo' laam.*	*Laam.*	*Tin tseng.*
黑色	老藍	藍	天青

Deep-blue.	Brown.	Carmine.	Carnation.
Un tseng.	*Tsung shik.*	*Kaam u hung.*	*Chik shik.*
元青	椶色	金魚紅	赤色

Crimson.	Green.	Pea-green.	Indigo.
In chi shik.	*Luk shik.*	*Tau tseng shik.*	*Yeung laam.*
胭脂色	綠色	豆青色	洋藍

Purple.	Orange.	Red.	Scarlet.
Sz'fan shik.	*Wong taan shik.*	*Hung shik.*	*Fa' hung.*
紫粉色	黃丹色	紅色	花紅

Snuff color.	White.	Ivory white.	Yellow.
Pi'in shik.	*Paak shik.*	*Nga wong shik.*	*Wong shik.*
臭烟色	白色	牙黃色	黃色

DIALOGUE ON GETTING A CHINA BOY.
Tsing sz tsai.
請事仔

Can you get me a good boy?
Ni tung ngo tsing tak yat ko' ho sz tsai 'm?'
你同我請得一個好事仔唔

How much will you pay him?
Ni pi ki toh yan kung kue?
你俾幾多人工佢

The same that other people pay.
Too hai pit' yan kom toh.
都係別人咁多

He wants $8.00 a month.
Kue iu pat ko ngan tsin yat ko uet.
佢要八個銀錢一個月

He ought to be satisfied with $6.00.
Yau luk ko kue too sum chuk la.
有六個佢都心足罅

Where was he employed last?
Kue sin yat tsoi pin chue tso kwoh?
佢先日在边處做過

He stopped with Mr.——— before.
Kue sin yat tsoi mi se chue.
佢先日在未士一處

How long did he stop with him?
Kue tsoi kue chue yau ki kau'?
佢在佢處有幾久

He stopped with him eighteen months.
Kue tsoi kue chue yau nin poon.
佢在佢處有年半

Why did he leave him?
Wai mat ye' kue 'm tso?

為乜野佢唔做

Because he got sick.
Yan wai kue tak peng'.

因為佢得病

Bring him here on Monday.
Lai pai yat kung kue loi.

礼拜一共佢耒

I think he is very stupid.
Ngo tai ta'k kue ngoo chun kwoh tau

我聽得佢愚蠢過頭

No, he is very smart.   Can he find security?
'M hai, kue ho tiu' tek ke'   Kue yau yan po' mo' ni?

唔係佢好跳踢嘅．佢有人保冇

I can secure him.
Ngo po' tak kue.

我保得佢

Tell him I will give him $6.00.
Wa' kue chi ngo pi luk ko ngan tsin kwoh kue.

話佢知我俾六个銀錢過佢

When I find him useful, I will give him more.
Ngo hon kwo . yau yung', Ngo tsau tim' toh tik.

我看過有用我就添多的

You must sleep in the house.   When shall I begin?
Ni pit iu tsoi hong fa'n.   Ngo ki shi hoi shau ni?

你必要在行瞓．我幾時開手呢

If you want to go out, you must ask me.
Ni hai iu shut kai : Ni pit iu man kwoh ugo.

你係要出街．你必要問過我

DIALOGUE ON GETTING A CHINA BOY.

Can you cook? Can you wash?
Ni nang tso` chue?* *Ni nang sai`i?

你能做厨. 你能洗衣

Light the fire. Sweep the rooms.
Tim cheuk foh`.* *So`kwoh ni ko fong.

点着火. 掃過呢个房

Wash the clothes. Wash the windows.
Sai`kwo ni tik i fok. *Sai kwoh ko tseung.*

洗過呢的衣服. 洗過个窓

Wash the floor. Sweep the stairs.
Sai`kwoh ni tik lau` pan *So lau.*

洗過呢的樓板. 掃樓

Trim the lamps. Brush my clothes.
Tsin lang`. *So kwoh ngo tiki fok.*

剪燈. 掃過我的衣服

Brush my hat. Knives and forks.
So kwoh ngo teng` mo.* *Cha` ka`p too tsai.

掃過我頂帽. 义反刀仔

Come at seven every morning.
Chiu chiu ni iu tsat tim chung loi.

朝朝你耍七点鐘来

Go home at eight every night.
Man` man` fan hue pat tim chung.

晚晚酱去八点鐘

You will take care of the baby.
Hi kung ngo ta` li tik sai mon tsai.

你共我打理的細吻仔

Take the baby out.
Kung kue chut hue kai wan`.

共佢出去街还

EVENING ORDERS.
Man tau fun fo.

晚頭吩咐

Snuff this candle.　　Put the light out.
Tsin ha' ni chi chuk.　Choi sik ni chi tang foh.'

剪吓呢枝燭．吹息呢枝燈火

This lamp is not clean.
Ni tsa'n tang 'm kon tsing.

呢盞燈唔乾净

The servant has washed it clean to-day.
Koon tim kom yat tsau sai ching.

管店今日就洗净

I think the oil is bad.
Ngo tai' ia'k ni tik yau 'm ho'.

我聽呢的油唔好

Has the servant shut all the windows?
Koon tim san' mai che ing mi?

管店閂埋窓未

Take care to bolt the doors.
Chi kan iu sheung moon cha'p.

至緊要上門揷

This lock is out of order.
Ni pa' so tso' wai lok.

呢把鎖做壞洛

Get this lock repaired.
Ching fa'n ni pa' soh!

整畚呢把鎖

He wants half a dollar to repair the lock.
Kue iu poon ko ngan tsin ching ni pa' soh.'

佢要半個銀錢整呢把鎖

EVENING ORDERS.

You better buy a new one.
Ni kang ho mai kwoh sam 'ko

你更好買過新佃

Please give me some money.
To` fan ni pi tik ngan kwoh ngo

多煩你俾的銀過我

I want some money besides.
Ngo ling ngoi iu tik ngan tim.

我另外要的銀添

What do you want money for?
Ni iu ngan tso mat ye´?

你要銀做乜野

I want it for to-morrow's expenses.
Ngo iu loi ming yat mai ye´.

我要耒明日買野

You charge too much for the things.
Ni tik ye´ hoi tak kwai kwoh tau.

你的野開得貴過頭

That is what I paid for it.
Ngo hai kom toh ngan mai ke`.

我係咁多銀買嘅

Go to bed just now.
Ni ha´ hue fan lok.

呢吓去瞓洛

Get up early to-morrow morning.
Ming yat tso shan hi shan.

明日早晨起身

Has the washerman brought my clothes?
Shai yi lo` nim fan ngo tik yi fuk loi?

洗衣佬拈番我的衣服耒

EVENING ORDERS.

Tell the washerman to send in his bill.
Kiu sai i lo` hoi ta`n loi.

叫洗衣佬開単夹

Have you made up your accounts?
Ni shuen tsing sho`'m tsang?

你算清数唔曾

Not yet.　　When can you let me have it?
'M tsang.　　Ni ki shi tsau pi tak kwo kur?

唔曾．你幾時就俾得過佢

Two days more.　　Has Mr.—— paid his money?
Chi leung yat tim`.　　Mi si——pi liu ngan mi?

遲兩日添．未士――俾了銀未

He will pay to-morrow
Kue ming yat tsau pi.

佢明日就俾

See that the money is weighed.
Iu hon kue toi kwo ni tik ngan.

要看過兌過呢的銀

If there is any thing short;
Yeuk hai 'm tak kau.

若係唔得够

I will make him pay the difference.
Ngo iu kue po tsuk.

我要佢補足

Pay this bill.　　Take his receipt.
Chi ni tiu ta`n.　　Kiu kue so` fan tiu shau ta`n.

支呢条単．叫佢寫番条收単

Put it in my own account.
Yap ngo ming` ha` sho`.

入我名下数

EVENING ORDERS.

Don't put it in the house account.
Mok yap kung sz sho.

莫入公司數

I have no money to pay this bill.
Ngo mo` ngan chi ni tiu` ta`n.

我冇銀支呢條單

I will give you a check on the bank.
Ngo pi yat cheung chik ni hue ngan hang shau.

我俾一張嘅你去銀行收

Can I pay this bill?   Don't pay it just now.
Ni tiu ta`n chi tak ngan mi?   Ni ha` 'm chi tak`.

呢條單支得銀未. 呢吓唔支得

I want to examine my accounts.
Ngo iu hon kwoh sho.

我要看過數

Shall I tell the bearer to come to-morrow?
Kom ngo wa` chi loi yan ming yat loi e`?

咁我話知來人明日來㖿

If you please.
To fan` ni lok.

多煩你嘞

What is the total of your accounts?
Ni chung shü ki toh?

你總數幾多

I don't know just now.   Is it correct?
Ngo ni ha` 'm chi.   Cheuk 'm cheuk?

我呢吓唔知. 着唔着

How many orders have you got?
Ni yau ki cheung a` ta` chi?

你有幾多張啞打紙

EVENING ORDERS.

I have not counted them.
Ngo mi yau shu' kwo.

我未有數過

You must file all these orders.
Ni pit iu chuen mai ni tik a' ta' chi.

你必要穿埋呢的唖打紙

Go over your accounts with Mr.———.
Ni hue tung mi si——— toi kwoh sho'

你去同末士――對過數

He says he is very busy.
Kue wa' kue ho` toh sze`.

佢話佢好多事

Do it when he has time.
Tang kue ha'n tsau toi.

等佢閒就對

I have gone over these accounts.
Ngo toi kwo ni tiu sho lok.

我對過呢条數洛

Do you find them correct?
Toi kwoh cheuk 'm ni?

對過着唔呢

There is ten dollars difference.
Tsang shap ko ngan tsin sho'.

掙十個銀錢數

Where is your counting board?
Ni suen poon tsoi pin chu?

你算盤在边處

Examine these accounts again carefully.
Siu sum suen kwoh ni tiu sho'.

小心算過呢条數

It is all right now. Square the old accounts.
Ni ha\` cheuk lok. *Suen ching kau sho'.*

呢吓着洛.算清舊数

Begin a fresh account to-day.
Kum yat hi kwoh sun sho

今日起過新数

Make up your accounts every week.
Ni ko ko lai pai iu suen sho

你个个礼拜要算数

You ought to be very particular.
Ni koi iu ching ching tso' tso'.

你該要清清楚楚

You mix up your accounts.
Ni ni' tik sho' tsung to\` luen.

你呢的数總倒亂

Put all the receipts on one side.
Loi sho' sheung mai yat pin.

来数上埋一边

Put the payments on another side.
Chi sho' sheung kwo yat pin.

支数上過一边

Deduct the payments from the receipts.
Cheung loi shu chu hue chi sho'.

将来数除去支数

You will know the balance on hand.
Ni tsau chi chuen shu mi ki toh.

你就知存数尾幾多

Put all the money into the treasury.
So' yau ngan leong fung yap ngan chong.

昕有銀両放入銀倉

FAMILIAR SENTENCES.
Tsuk wa'.

俗話.

Bring me a basin of water.
Chow yat poon shui loi.

抽一盤水耒

Why is this water so dirty?
Wai mat ye' ni tik shui kom o' tso?

Go and change it.
Hue u'n kwoh kue.

為乜野呢的水咁污漕.去換過佢

Bring me some hot water.
Nim tik yit shui loi.

I want to shave.
Ngo iu t'hai soo.

拈的熱水耒．我要剃鬚

Call the barber.
Kiu tai tau lo loi.

Make some tea.
Chung pooi cha'.

叫剃頭佬耒．沖杯茶

Where is my hat?
Ngo ting mo tsoi pin chu.

Brush my coat.
Tsat tsing ngo kin sham.

我頂帽在边處．擦净我件衫

I am going out.
Ngo ni ha' iu tsut kai.

I will come back soon.
Ngo tsau fan loi.

我呢吓要出街.我就番耒

Send this letter to Mr.———.
Nim ni cheung shun hu——— chu.

Wait for an answer.
Tang hoi yam.

拈呢張信去——處．等回音

Has the servant come back?
Koon tim fan loi mi?

管店番耒未

Not yet.
'M tsang.

The servant has come back.
Koon tim fan loi lok.

唔 曽．管店番耒洛

FAMILIAR SENTENCES.

Mr. ——— is not at home.
Mi see m tsoi ka'.

未士－－唔在家

Tell him to go back again.　　Come back quick.
Kiu' kue tsoi hue kwoh　　*Fai tik fan loi.*

呌佢再去過．快的畨耒

Don't wait long.
Mok 'ung' kom kow.

莫等咁久

The servant has given the letter to him.
Koon tim kau liu sun kwoh kue.

管店交了信過佢

What did he say?　　He will send an answer just now.
Kue tim wa'?　　*Kue chow pi hoi yam.*

佢点話．佢就俾回音

Did you see him?　　What is he doing?
Ni kin kue 'm tsang?　　*Kue tsoi chu' tso' mat ye'?*

你見佢唔曾．佢在處做乜野

He is talking with a gentleman.
Kue tung yan hak kung shurt wa'

佢同人客講說話

Show me the house.　　Send this card in.
Chi chi kan uk kwoh ngo　　*Nim ni ko tip yap hue.*

指知間屋過我．拈呢个帖入去

Ask the gentleman to step in.
Tsing yan hak yap loi.

請人客入耒

Bring a chair here.　　Open the venetians.
Nim yat cheung i loi.　　*Ta' hoi ngau pak ip cheung.*

拈一張椅耒．打開牛柏葉窓

FAMILIAR SENTENCES.

BREAKFAST.

Is breakfast ready?   Breakfast is ready.
Tso` cha' pin 'm chang?*   *Tso` cha' pin lok.

早茶便唔曾．早茶便洛

Invite that gentleman to come to breakfast.
Tsing ni wai yan hak loi shik chiu' cha'n.

請呢位人客耒食朝餐

Take off the dish covers.
Kit hi koh tip koi.

揭起个碟盖

Give this plate to that gentleman.
Pi ni koh tip kwoh ni wai yan hak.

俾呢个碟過呢位人客

Easy, easy; or Take care.
Shun shun; or siu' sam.

順順．又曰小心．

Bring the eggs here.   Take this plate away.
Ning ko tik kai tan loi.   *Ning ni ko tip hoi hue.*

擰个的鷄蛋耒．擰呢个碟開去

Change this napkin.   Pass this dish round.
Oon chuen ni tiu po` tsai.   *Cheung ni ko tip chuen kwoh hue.*

換轉呢条布仔．將呢个碟傳過

Put the curry on the table.
Fong poon ka'fe'choi toi min.

放盤㗎啡在枱面

Did you prepare any toast?
Ni yau hong ting to` se' 'm tsang

你有炕定多時唔曾

FAMILIAR SENTENCES.   33

Give me a cup of tea.　　The tea is too strong.
Pi yat pooi cha` kwoh ngo.　Ni tik cha` hung kwoh tau.

俾一杯茶過我、呢的茶濃過頭

Get some more water.　　Put more tea in the teapot.
Chung tik shui tim.　　Fong toh tik cha` ip lok cha` hoo

冲的水添、放多的茶葉落茶壺

Pass the milk to that gentleman.
Ning` ni tik ngau yu kwo ni wai yan hak.

擰呢的牛乳過呢位人客

Which gentleman?　The one opposite to me.　Put some milk into the tea.
Pin wai yan hak?　Ngo tooi min ni wai.　Chung tik ngau yu lok cha` chue.

边位人客、我對面呢位、冲的乳落茶處

Remove the table cloth.　　Enquire about dinner.
Shau toi po`.　　Man tai` tsan moon.

收枱布、問大餐門

Sir, what will you have for dinner to-day?
Sz tau ni iu mat ye`; kom yat tso tai` chan?

事頭你要乜野今日做大餐

Make me a pigeon pie.　　Roast a capon.
Tso` yat poon pak kop min kwai.　Shiu yat chik sin kai.

做一盤白鴿麵龜、燒一隻剒雞

Make some curry.　　Don't make it too hot.
Tso` yat poon ka` li.　'M ho tso kom` lat.

做一盤喫唎、唔好做咁辣

What kind of curry, sir?　　Can you get any oysters?
Tso` mat ye` ka` li ni?　Mai tik to ho` mani?

做乜野喫唎呢、買得到蠔唔呢

I can't get it; there is none in the market.
'M mai tak to`; kai si mo tak mai.

唔買得到、街市冇得賣

FAMILIAR SENTENCES.

Get some good vegetables. Are there any oysters in the market?
Mai tik ho tsing tsoi. *Kai si yau ho` mai mo ni?*

買的好青菜 街市有蠔賣冇呢

Buy a piece of good beef. Make some soup.
Mai yat fai ho` ngau yuk.*  *Tso` tik tong.

買一塊好牛肉 做的湯

Tell the cook to make it properly.
Fan foo tso` chue lo tso` ho tik.

吩咐做厨佬做好的

Three gentlemen dine with me to-day.
Yau sam wai yan hak loi sik tai` chan'.

有三位人客来食大餐

Don't spoil the soup. Try some plantains.
Mok tso` wai ni poon tong. *Chau tik tsiu.*

莫做壞呢盤湯 燂的蕉

Cover it with butter. Get some cabbages.
Cha` min liu.*  *Mai tik ye` tsoi.

搽麵料 買的耶菜

Do you want it cooked?
Ni iu ching shuk kue `m ni?

尔要整熟佢唔呢

Cook a boned chicken. Kill this capon.
Lung yat chik toi kwat kai. *Tong ni chik sin kai.*

弄一隻退骨鷄 劏呢隻𤞚鷄

Get it roasted. Do you want it roasted to-day?
Ning hue shiu. *Ni iu kom yat shiu mo?*

擰去燒 你要今日燒嚤

Can you do so? I am afraid I can not.
Ni tso` tak `m ni? *Ngo pah `m tso` tak.*

尔做得唔呢 我怕唔做得

Well, put it off till to-morrow.	Ho le̔ lau fan ming yat le̔.	好喱留番明日喱
Hang it up.	Tiu hi kue.	吊起佢
Make it tender.	Tsʽ sung kue.	做鬆佢
Prepare fowl cutlets.	Tsò kat lit kai.	做咭唎鷄
Roast a leg of mutton.	Shiu yat pi yeung yuk.	燒一胚羊肉
Don't over do it.	Mok shiu suk kwo tau.	莫燒熟過頭

LUNCH.

Lunch is on the table, sir.
Shiu sik fong tsoi toi min lok.
小食放在枱面咯

Very well.	Ho le̔.	好厘
I will come just now.	Ngo tsau loi.	我就耒
What have you got?	Yau mat ye̔ ni?	有乜野呢
A roast fowl.	Yat chek siu kai.	一隻燒鷄
Some cold meat.	Yau tik tong yuk.	有的凍肉
Get a bottle of beer.	Ning̔ yat tsun pi tsau̔ loi.	擰一樽啤酒耒
There is no more beer.	Mò pi tsau lok.	冇啤酒咯
Go to —— and get some.	Hue —— chue lo̔ tik.	去一處取的
Please give me a note.	Tò fan pʽ jat cheung sun kwo ngo.	多煩俾一張信過我
Give me a tumbler of water.	Pi yat pooi shui kwo ngo.	俾一杯水過我

DINNER.

Dinner is ready, sir.	Tai̔ tsʽan pin lok.	大餐便洛
Is it on the table?	Fong tsoi toi min 'm tsang?	放在枱面唔曾
Invite the gentleman to take his seat.	Tsing yan hak tsò toi.	請人客坐枱
Remove the soup tureen.	Ning hoi ni ko tong tau.	擰開呢的湯斗
Bring the roast beef.	Ning shiu ngau yuk loi.	擰燒牛肉耒

Bring that dish of sauce. This beef is roasted rare.
Ning ni chung chap loi. *Ni tik ngau yuk shiu tak̆ shang.*

擰呢盅汁耒 呢的牛肉燒得生

Please carve that capon.
To fa`n ni kot hoi ni chik sin kai.

多煩你割開呢隻刣雞

This fowl is not thoroughly done.
Ni chek kai ``m tsang shiu tak̆ tau.

呢隻雞唔曾燒得透

Tell the cook to roast it better next time.
Kiu tso` chue tai ye` tsz shiu ho` tik.

叫做厨第二次燒好的

Open a bottle of sherry. Don't break the cork.
Hoi yat tsun che` li tsau. *Mok tso lan ni ko tsun chat.*

開一罇車厘酒 莫做爛呢個樽橍

Don't shake the bottle. Pour the wine into the decanter.
Mok yeung ni ko tsun. *To` ni tik tsau lok pak tsau tsun.*

莫挟呢個罇 倒呢的酒落白酒樽

This wine glass is not clean. Clean this wine glass.
Ni ko tsau pooi `m kon tsing`. *Tsŏ tsing ni ko tsau pooi.*

呢個酒杯唔乾净 做净呢個酒杯

It suits my taste. The cook is very strange.
Hop ngo hau mi. *Ni ko tso`chue lo` chun koo kwai.*

合我口味 呢個做厨佬真古怪

He cooks very well sometimes. This curry is very nice.
Yau si kue tso tak̆ ki` ho.* *Ni tik ka` li tsun hai ho.

有時佢做得幾好 呢的架唎真係好

Sometimes he spoils the dishes.
Yau shi kue tsŏ wai ni tik tsoi.

有時佢做壞呢的菜

FAMILIAR SENTENCES.

Why don't you get me some oysters?
Tsò mat ni 'm mai tik hò ngo shik?

做乜你唔買的蠔我食

There is none in the market.   Did you buy any fruit?
Kai si mo tak mai.   Ni yau shang kwo mai to 'm tsang?

街市冇得賣．你有生菓買到唔曾

Yes, I have got three kinds.   What have you got besides?
Yau lok, ngo mai sam yeung.   Ni wan yau mat yé tim?

有洛．我買三樣尔還有乜野添

There is a peach tart.   Bring it on the table.
Yau yat ko tò tsai tart.   Ning loi fong tsoi toi min.

有一個桃仔噠．擰來放在枱面

Put the fowl in the safe.   Give it to the dog.
On ni shik kai tsoi shá fong ting chue.   Pi kwo kau shik.

安呢隻鷄在沙風燈處俾過狗食

TEA.—Make the tea ready at 6 o'clock. Tell the cook to fry some pancakes.
Lok tim chung tsò pin chá.   Kiu tsò chue lò hong tik pan kik.

六點鐘做便茶呌做厨佬烘的班戟

Don't burn them.   He did very bad the last time.
Mok hong tsiú.   Kue sin wooi tso tak shap fan 'm ho.

莫烘焦．佢先回做得十分唔好

I want to cut his wages.
Ngo sheung cheuk kot kue yan kung lok.

我想着割佢人工㖞

Bring the tea canister here.
Ning ni ko chá ip tsun loi.

擰呢個茶葉樽來

Take the lid off.   What kind of tea is it?
Kit hoi koi.   Ni tik hai mat yé chá?

揭開盖．呢的係乜野茶

This is Souchong tea.
Ni tik hai siu chong.

呢 的 係 小 種

This tea is very bad.
Ni tik cha' shap fan 'm ho.

呢 的 茶 十 分 唔 好

That is the best I can get.
Ngo mai ni tik sun chi ho ke' lok.

我 買 呢 的 算 至 好 嘅 洛

Do you mean to say so?　　How dare I to tell a lie?
Ni kom wa' haichan ke'?　Ngo tim kom kung tai wa'?

你 咁 話 係 真 嘅．我 点 敢 講 大 話

Try and get some good tea.　　I will enquire to-morrow.
Shi ha' mai ti': ho cha'.　Ngo ming yat hue man kwoh.

試 吓 買 的 好 茶．我 明 日 去 問 過

I like strong tea.　　Mrs. ——— likes weak tea.
Ngo chung i'yam yung cha'.　A' ne'ung tsai chung i'yam tam cha'.

我 中 意 飲 濃 茶．亞 娘 仔 中 意 飲 淡 茶

Put some more sugar into the tea.
Fong toh tik tong lok cha' chue.

放 多 的 糖 落 茶 處

Make some coffee just now.
Ni ha' tso tik ka' fe'.

呢 吓 做 的 㗎 啡

If you have no coffee, prepare a little chocolate.
Hai mo ka' fe', ching tik chue ko lat.

係 冇 㗎 啡 整 的 啫 咕 聿

Bring another tea saucer.　　Remove the tea tray.
Ning kwo yat chik cha' tip.　Tsau cha' poon hoi hue.

擰 過 一 隻 茶 碟．抽 茶 盤 開 去

BUSINESS CONVERSATION.

Have you any good table rice?   Yes, but it is very dear.
Ni yau tik shè ung pak mai mo` ni˝?   *Yau, tsung hai kwai che˝.*

你有的上白米冇呢．有總係貴嗻

What do you mean by dear?   Four dollars a picul.
Tim yeung wai chi kwai ni.   *Sì ko ngan tsin yat ta˝m.*

点樣為之貴呢．四個銀錢擔

I don't want a picul.   I want fifty pounds.
Ngo `m iu˝ yat tam.   *Ngo iu˝ ng shap pong.*

我唔要一擔．我要五十石旁

I sell it three cents a pound.   Is that the lowest price?
Mooi pong sam ko sin si.   *Hai kung tò ka˝ tsin `m.*

每磅三个先士．係公道價錢唔

I want some preserves and pickles.   That is what I want.
Ngo iu˝ tik tong ko sun kwo˝.   *Ngo tsing hai iu˝ ni lik.*

我要的糖菓酸果我正係要呢的

How much a dozen?
Ki toh ngan yat ko ta˝ sun.

幾多銀一個打臣

Send three dozen to my house.
Shai yan sung sam ko ta˝ sun tò ngo uk.

使人送三個打臣到我屋

What is the price of sugar?   What quality do you want?
Tong mat ye ka` tsin ni?   *Ni iu˝ pin tang ke˝*

糖乜野價錢呢．尒要边等嘅

I want the best sugar.   Do you mean sugar candy?
Ngu iu˝ chi ho ke˝ tong.   *Hai iu˝ ping fa˝ `m hai*

我要至好嘅糖．係要氷花唔係

Sugar candy sells at twelve cents a pound.
Ping fa˝ mai shap i ko sin si yat pong.

氷花賣十二個先士一磅

I want some flour too.　　I have no American flour.
Ngo iu⸍ tik min⸜ fun tim.　　Ngo mo⸜ fa⸍ ki min⸜.

我要的麵粉添　我有花旗麵

I have some good China flour.　　I don't want it.
Ngo yau tik ho⸜ poon ti min⸜.　　Ngo ⸜m iu⸍ ko tik.

我有的好本地麵　我唔要佢的

I am very sorry.　　I can not accommodate you with it.
Ngo kin ⸜m ho⸜ i sz.　　Ngo ⸜m ching yau tak fung.

我見唔好意思　我唔曾有得奉

Very well, let me go to the next door ;
Ho⸜ ni tang ngo kwo lak li po ;

好呢等我過隔離舖

And see whether I can get it :
Sz ha⸍ hon chi mai tak to⸍ ⸜m ;

試吓看知買得倒唔

And I will come back ;　　To buy some other things from you.
In hau fan⸍ loi ;　　Tung ni mai tik ye⸍ tim.

然後番来　同你買的野添

Thank you ; Good bye.
To che⸍ ni lok ching le⸍.

多謝尔洛請嘑

Please let me take your name.
To fa⸜n ni tung chi ming ngo ho⸜ lok po⸜.

多煩尔通知名我好落簿

Where do you live, sir ?
Tsuen ka⸍ tsoi pin chu⸍ chu⸜ ni.

尊駕在边處住呢

When shall I send the bill to you ?　　Any time you please.
Ki shi ngo sung tan to⸜ ni chu⸜ ni.　　Yum nishishi too ho⸜.

幾時我送單到你處呢　𦲷尔時時
　　　　　　　　　　　　　　都好

TRAVELER'S CONVERSATION. 41

Oh! how beautiful!   What a magnificent view!
Ah ki ho' chi`!*    *Kom`ho ho' tai ah!

呀. 幾 好 緻. 咁 好 浩 大 嚛

Did you ever see any thing like it?
Ni kin yau mat che' tak kue ke' ni?

尔 見 有 乜 似 得 佢 嘅 呢

No sir; I never saw any thing so beautiful.
Mo; Ngo mi tsangkin kwo yau kom` ho' ke'.

無. 我 未 曾 見 過 有 咁 好 嘅

I should like to live here all my life.
Ngo chung i'shi shi ehue tsoi ni chue` lok.

我 中 意 時 時 住 在 呢 處 咯

I would not; 'tis too far from the city.
Ngo `m tak; li fau uen kwo tau.

我 唔 得. 離 埠 遠 過 頭

You can go to the city by railroad in two days.
Ni taap fo' che' hue fau le'ung yat tsau` tak lok.

尔 搭 火 車 去 埠 兩 日 就 得 咯

Have you such beautiful scenery in your country?
Ni kwok chong yau yu tsz'king che'ung yau mo` ni.

尔 國 中 有 如 此 景 像 有 冇 呢

No. I think we have nothing like it.
Mo`, Ngo tai ngo ti` mo` yu tsz` ke'.

無. 我 睇 我 地 冇 如 此 嘅

I enjoy traveling through such scenery.
Ngo lok yu yau woon **tszè king**.

我 樂 於 遊 玩 此 景

So I would, if the coach did not shake me so much.
Ngo to` ooi tan'g yeuk fai che`m sai kom` iu'.

我 都 噲 倘 若 快 車 唔 使 咁 搖

Well, you will not have long to suffer.
Ho lok, ni `m shai sau kom̀ noi fo`o lok.

好咯，尔唔使受咁耐苦咯

We will get to N—— very soon.
Ngo ti` che`ung loi yau hue —— shap fa`n fai lok.

我地將来遊去一十分快咯

Is this the right road to N——?
Ni tiu` lo` hai hue pa`k pi`n ke `m hai ni——?

呢條路係去比便嘅唔係呢

Yes, it is. No, you are on the wrong road.
Hai lok. Ni tiu lo` `m hai tsok lok.

係咯．呢條路唔係錯咯

You go back one mile, then turn to the right.
Ni ha`ng chuen ta`u yat mai lo` in hau chuen kwo yau pin tsau hop

尔行轉頭一咪路然後轉過右便就合

Will you let me ride with you? Yes, you may, I have a light load.
Ni ha`ng tung ngo ma` che` hue? Ho ni, ni ka` hing che` chi.

尔肯同我馬 車去好呢尔架輕車啫

Let us go and hire a horse and buggy.
Ngo ti` hue ching ka` ma` che` ni.

我地去請駕馬車呢

I would rather go on horseback. Very well; 'tis all the same to me.
Ngo ming yuen ke` ma` hue lok. Ho ah ngo to` yat ye`ung chi.

我寧愿騎馬去咯好哑我都一樣啫

We can hire two saddle horses just as well.
Ngo ti ching leung tseak yau on ke` to` hai yat ye`ung che`.

我地請兩隻有鞍嘅都係一樣啫

How much will he charge per day?
Ki lo`h ngan yat yat` ni.

幾多銀一日呢

He says we can have them for ten dollars.
Kue wa′ ni mooi yat shap ko` ngan tsin t⸺ ta′k lok.

佢話呢.每日十個銀錢就得咯

That's too much. I will not pay that.
Iu kom` toh ngan ngo `m pi ta′k.

要咁多銀我唔俾得

How much do you want to give?　　Six dollars is enough.
Ni se′ung pi ki toh ni.　　*Lok ko` ngan tsin ho lok.*

你想俾幾多呢.六個銀錢好咯

He says he can't let us have them at that price.
Kue wa′ ko ko ka′ tsin `m tso` ta′k.

佢話個個價錢唔做得

He says the roads are very bad just now.
Kue wa′ kom` ha` ko tiu` lo shap fa′n sam.

佢話今下個條路十分甚

Then let us wait till next week.
In hau` ta′ng to tai i ko lai pai chi lok.

然後等到第二個禮拜至囉

Very well!　All right.　Very good!　Let us go back to our hotel.
Ho-ni!　*Hop lo`k.*　*Ho` lok!*　*Fa′n hue haak ue` ni.*

好呢.合咯.好咯.番去客寓呢

No, let us take a walk first.　Which way shall we go?
`M ho, ha′ng ha′ tim chi lok.*　*Hue pin chue` ni?

唔好.行吓添至囉.去边處呢

Let us go down that way.　Wait a moment; I'm not ready yet.
Lo`k ko` chue a′h.　*Ta′ng yat tsan ngo mi tak pi`.*

落個處吔.等一陣我未得備

Hurry up—I can't wait any more.　Make haste—'tis getting late!
Fai tik lok.　Ngo `m tang tak tim lok.　*Se′ung tik lok.　Chi lok.*

快的囉我唔等得添囉爽的囉遲咯

ON MEETING A FRIEND.

Where do you come from?   Where have you been this long time?
Ni yau pin` chue loi`?   *Mat ni hue kom`noi` hue pin chue`?*

尔由边處来． 凡尔去咁耐去边處

I have been working at the Mission. Could you not come to town every night?
Ngo hue Mi shun ta` kung loi`.   *Ni `man` ma`n `m mai fa`n?*

我去尾臣打工来 尔晚晚唔埋埠

No sir; I could not; it is too far.
`M ta`k. Ngo `m tak ke` tai `uen` ah.

唔得．我唔得嘅太遠哑

How far is it from here to your place?
Yau ni chue` hue ni chue` yau ki `uen ni?

由呢處去尔處有幾遠呢

I think it is about three miles.   Do you like living at the Mission?
Ngo tai to` yau sa`m mai lo`.*    *Ni chong i tsoi Mi shun chue`.

我睇都有三哩路．你中意在尾臣住

Yes, I like it very well for the present.
Hai, ngo kum ha` kin to` ki ho kom.

係．我今下見都幾好咁

Are you working for an American?
Ni tsoi fa` ki` yan chue ta` kung?

尔在花旗八處打工

Yes sir; a gentleman who treats me very well.
Hai; ko sz tau toi tak ngo shap fa`n ho

係．伺事頭待得我十分好

Will you stay here this evening?
Kom ma`n ni chong tsoi ni chue`?

今晚尔重在呢處

No sir; I cannot; I must return at ten o'clock.
`M hai. Ngo `m tak ngo si pit shap tim chong fa`n hue

唔係．我唔得我是必十点鐘返去

THE SCHOOL.

Why did you not come last night?
Tso mat ni ʼuok maan mʻ loi?

做乜尔昨晚唔耒．

Why do you not come to school?
Wai ho ni ʼm loi tuk sz?

為何尔唔耒讀書

Why do you not come every day?
Wai ho ni ʼm yat yat loi?

為何尔唔日日耒．

Are you busy all the time?
Hai ni shi shi tō m tukʻ han?

係尔時時都唔得閒

What book do you study now?
Ni in haʻ tuk mat yeʻ sz?

尔現下讀乜野書

Where did you learn to read?
Ni tsoi pin chu hak ooi tuk keʻ?

尔在邊處學噲讀嘅

Who taught you?
Sui yan kaw ni keʻ?

誰人教尔嘅．

How many months have you attended school?
Ni tuk liuʻ ki toh ko uet sz.

尔讀了幾多个月書

I make very little progress in Chinese.
Ngo to ʻm toh hak takʻ ki toh tung waʻ.

我都唔多學得幾多唐話

I have not much time to study.
Ngo mo mat shi hau puk chaup.

我無乜時候學習

How did you enjoy yourself?
Ni shap fan fai lok haʻ?

尔十分快樂呀

I have an engagement.
Ngo yau tik sz kohn.

我有的事幹

Do you wish to come to school?
Ni chong i loi tuk sz?

尔中意耒讀書．

Is your father living in this city?
Ni ko foo tsan tsoi poon fau chueʻ?

尔伲父親在本埠處

THE SCHOOL.

Have you any brothers?
Ni yau hing tai yau mo?

What is your business?
Ni tsò mat yè shang i`?

尔有兄弟有無. 尔做乜野生意

I want to see you to-morrow at ten o'clock.
Ngo iu ming yat shap tim chong kin ha` ni.

我要明日十点鐘見吓你

How much do you get a month?
Ni yat ko uet yau ki toh ngan yan kung?

尔一侗月有幾多銀人工

We need a fire to-night.
Ngo ti um muan iu' fat cheuk koh foh lo.

我地今晚要發着侗火爐

Is the room warm enough?
Ni ko fong nune 'm ni?

呢侗房暖唔呢

The streets are very muddy.
Ko lik kai toh shap fan sam nai paan..

佢的街道十分深泥溼

Will you take a lesson this morning?
Ni Km` chiu tuk ni sau sz 'm?

尔今朝讀呢首書唔

Do you understand your lesson?
Ni shik tak kai ni ko sau sz 'm tsang?

尔識得解尔侗冇書唔曾

Do you speak English often in your store?
Ni shi shı tsoi po yau kong fan wa' yau mo`?

尔時時在舖有講蕃話有無

Every body say the same thing.
Yan yan to hai kom wa`.

At what time does your teacher come?
Ni ko sin shang ki shı loi`.

人人都係咁話. 尔侗先生幾時来

THE SCHOOL.

You do not know your lesson.
Ni 'm hiu tak' luk ni sau sz.

Do you make much progress?
Ni hok tak ho toh?

尔唔曉得讀呢首書. 尔學得好多

No, I do not, my memory is not good.
Ngo too 'm kin kung ke. Ngo 'm ho ki sing.

我都唔見工嘅. 我唔好記性

My pronunciation is good, but not my memory.
Ngo how kim ki ho; wai hai mo ki sing.

我口鉗幾好. 惟係無記性

I make some progress in writing.
Ngo se tsze kin tik kong.

No, I think I do not make any progress.
Ngo tai ngo toh 'm kin mat kong.

我寫字見的工. 我睇我都吾見乜工

I study as much as I can.
Ngo tuk tak kom' toh tuk kom' toh.

我讀得咁多讀咁多

I am more idle than studious.
Ngo laan toh kwo tuk sz.

Why do you come so soon?
Mat ni kom' tso' loi?

我懶多過讀書. 乜尔咁早来

I told you to come at one o'clock.
Ngo wa kwo ni chi yat tim chong loi loh.

我話過你知一点鐘来咯

Are you making money?
Ni yau tsin chan' mo?

尔有錢賺無

Where did you learn the language?
Ni tsoi pin chue hak wa' ke'?

尔在边處學話嘅

At home.　　In China.　　In this city.
Tsoi uk ki.　Tsoi tung san.　Tsoi ni ko fau.

在屋企. 在唐山. 在呢個埠.

THE SCHOOL.

How long did you study it?
Ni hok yau ki noi ah?

尔學有幾耐唖

I have studied, altogether, three years.
Ngo chung kung hak liu sam` nin.

我總共學了三年

Only three years?
Sam` nin chong`?

三年咗

Not more than three years.
Pat kwo sam nin hoi.

不過三年外

I commenced to study it in 1860.
Ngo yat tsin pat pak lok shap` nin hi sa`y hok

我一仟八百六十年起手學

I have studied a few months at a time.
Ngo ko shi hok tak` ki ko uet.

我伵時學得幾伵月

You have made good progress.
Ni chun ho toh kung lok.

尔進好多工咯

Do you think so?
Ni kin hai?

尔見係

Certainly; you speak as well as I do.
Kok sat hai; ni kung lak` ngo yat yeung lok.

碻實係尔講得我一樣

SHORT SENTENCES.

What is that? Be still. Speak louder.
Ni tik` hai` mat ye´? *Mok tsut sing´.* *Tai sing´ kung.*

呢的係乜野. 莫出聲. 大聲講

Stand up. Sit still. Come here. I am busy.
Ki hi san´. *Ching ching tso´ lok.* *Loi ni chue.* *Ngo yau sz.*

企起身. 靜靜坐落. 来呢處. 我有事

Where are you going? I can not tell you.
Ni hue pin chue? *Ngo `m wa´ tak` kwo ni chi`.*

你去边處. 我唔話得過你知

What for? Who are you? I am sick.
Wai mat sz? *Ni hai mat shui?* *Ngo yau peng´.*

為乜事. 你係乜誰. 我有病

I don't know you. Are you well?
Ngo `m sik tak` ni *Ni ho a´?*

我唔識得你 你好啞

He has made his fortune. Don't say so.
Kue fa´t liu` tai tsoi.* *`M ho kom´ wa`.

佢發了大財. 唔好咁話

Wait a little. What news? Are you sure?
Tang yat shi kan`. *Yau mat sun mun?* *Ni chi tak tsan mo´?*

等一時間. 有乜新聞. 你知得真嗎

The mail steamer has arrived. Where is he?
Sz sun foh suen toh liu`. *Kue tsoi pin chue?*

書信火船到了. 佢在边處

I am not quite sure. I don't know.
Ngo `m hai shap fa´n tsan´.* *Ngo `m chi.

我唔係十分真. 我唔知

He has gone to Canton. When is he coming back? Who says so?
Kue hue liu` Kwong tsau sing´. *Kue kishifan loi?* *Mat shui wa´?*

佢去了廣州城. 佢幾時番来. 乜誰話

SHORT SENTENCES.

Get out of the way. Don't speak with me. I don't care. Go and ask him.
Hang hoi la´. Mok tung ngo kung. Ngo `m li´. Ni hue man` kue.

行開嚟. 莫同我講. 我唔理. 你去問佢

He won't listen to me. I can not help it.
Kue `m teng´ ngo kung. Ngo to mo noi hoh.

佢 唔 聽 我 講. 我都無奈何

Send for him. He will not come.
Sai yan kiu kue loi. Kue `m ha´ng loi`.

使 人 呌 佢 耒. 佢 唔 肯 耒

He must come. I want this.
Kue pit iu loi. Ngo iu ni tik´.

佢 必 要 耒. 我 要 呢 的

You can not take it. What do you want?
Ni `m nim tak´. Ni iu mat ye´?

你 唔 拈 得. 你 要 乜 野

Who gives you permission? Help me.
Mat shui pi chu i`ni? Pong´ tso ngo.

乜 誰 俾 主 意. 你 幫 助 我

I want you to go with me. Never mind.
Ngo iu ni tung ngo hue. `M sai.

我 要 你 同 我 去. 唔 使

Open the door. Shut the window. Bring a chair.
Hoi moon`. Shan cheung´. Ta´m cheung yi loi.

開 門. 門 窓. 擔 張 椅 耒

Bring a light. Bring a cigar. What is your name?
Tim´ foh loi. Nim hau in loi. Ni kiu mat ming´?

點 火 耒. 拈 口 烟 耒. 你 呌 乜 名

Where do you belong? How old are you?
Ni hai` pin chue yan? Ni ki toh soi?

你 係 边 處 人. 你 幾 多 歲

SHORT SENTENCES.

Who sends you here?   That is right.
Mat shui kiu' ni loi?   *Hop lok.*

乜誰咩你来．合啱

It is not so.   Bring it here.   He struck me.
'M hai kom'.   *Nim loi ni chue.*   *Kue ta' ngo.*

唔係咁．拈来呢處．佢打我

Don't be afraid.   What shall I do?   Get up quick.   Put on your jacket.
'M pa'.   *Tim yeung ho ni?*   *Fai tik hi san'.*   *Cheuk fan' sam'.*

唔怕．点樣好呢．快的起身．着畨衫

Go just now.   Do it now.   He is dead.
Ni ha' hue.   *Ni ha' tso.*   *Kue sz liu.*

呢吓去．呢吓做．佢死了

When will he come?   When can you do it?
Kue kishi tsau loi?   *N' kishi tso' tak'?*

佢幾時就来．你幾時做得

I am hungry.   Go and buy some cakes.
Ngo to' hoh.   *Hue mai tik peng' loi'.*

我肚餓．去買的餅来、

Are you ready?   I am sleepy.
Ni chai pi 'm tsang?   *Ngo ngan fan'.*

你齊備唔曾，我眼瞓

I have lost a dollar.   Go and find it.
Ngo 'm kin liu yat ko nyan tsin.   *Hue cham' cheuk kue.*

我唔見了一個銀錢．去尋着佢

I don't know where it is.   Can he read?
Ngo 'm chi tsoi pin chue.   *Kue sik tsze mo?*

我唔知在边處．佢識字嗎

Come to-morrow.   I will give you an answer.
Ni ming yat loi.   *Ngo pi sing' yi ni.*

你明日来、我俾聲氣你

SHORT SENTENCES.

| How do you know? | I have seen it. | What does he say? | I am deaf. |
| Ni tim tak` chi` | Ngo kin kwo. | Kue wa` mat ye`? | Ngo yi lung. |

你點得知. 我見過. 佢話乜野. 我耳聾

| Wash your hands. | Don't be lazy. | Give it to me. | Let me see. |
| Sai shau. | `M ho lan`. | Pi kwo ngo. | Pi ngo hon. |

洗　手. 唔好懶. 彼過我. 彼我看

| Where shall I put it? | Don't spill it. |
| Ngo fong pin chue ho`? | Mok lau tsui`. |

我放边處好. 莫留出

| This is hard work. | I can't understand. |
| Ni tik hai san` foo kung foo`. | Ngo `m hiu tak`. |

呢的係辛苦工夫. 我唔曉得

| Why don't you come sooner? | I will go this evening. |
| Ni tso mat `m tso tik` loi? | Ngo kom man` tau hue. |

你做乜唔早的耒. 我今晚就去

| I have cut my finger. | Go and call the docter. |
| Ngo kut tsan shau tsi. | Hue kiu i shang loi. |

我割親手指. 去叫醫生耒

| I think so too. | I suppose so. |
| Ngo too hai kom` seung. | Ngo koo hai kom`. |

我都係咁想. 我估係咁

| Mind your own business. | I don't believe it. |
| Ni ta` li ni chi ki` shi. | Ngo `m sun. |

你打理你自己事. 我唔信

| You will know very soon. | What are you laughing at? |
| Ni chi ha tsau chi`. | Ni siu mat ye? |

你遲吓就知. 你笑乜野

| It is not yet finished. | Do it again. | Where are you employed? |
| Mi tso tak` he`. | Tsoi tso kwoh. | Ni tsoi pin chue ta` kung`. |

未做得起. 再做過. 你在边處打工

SHORT SENTENCES.

You ought not to do so.
Ni 'm koi kom' yung tso.
尔唔該咁樣做

It is very hot to-day.
Kom yat shap fan' yi't.
今日十分熱

I have forgotten it.
Ngo 'm ki tak'.
我唔記得

When does he sail?
Kue ki shi hang shuen?
佢幾时行船．

I have taken physic.
Ngo shik liu yuk.
我食了藥

Do you smoke?
Ni shik in mo'?
你食烟嗎．

He did it purposely.
Kue yau i tso ke'.
佢有意做嘅

Who is wrong?
Mat shui tso'?
乜誰錯

Pick this up.
Ch.ip fan' ni tik ye'.
執番呢的野

We move to-morrow.
Ngo tik ming yat poon uk.
我地明日搬屋

Don't break these things.
Mok ta' lan' ni tik' ye'.
莫打爛呢的野．

What time is it now?
Ni ha' ki to tim chong?
呢吓幾多点鐘

Who made this?
Ni tik hai mat shui tso ke'?
呢的係乜誰做嘅

It is very well made.
Tso' tak' shap fan' ho.
做得十分好

I did not say so.
Ngo mi yau kom' wa'.
我未有咁話．

He comes too late.
Kue to tak che'.
佢到得遲

He has just gone.
Kue tsau hue liu.
佢就去了．

That is not true.
Ni tik suet wa' 'm hai tsan' ke'.
呢的説話唔係真嘅

Did you call him?
Ni kiu kue lok?
你呌佢囉．

It is true.
Hai tsan' ke'.
係真嘅．

Every body knows it.
Yan yan to' chi.
人人都知

He has gone on board
Kue hoi liu' shuen.
佢開了船．

He has gone on shore.
Kue mai liu kai'.
佢埋了街．

He is an honest man.
Kue hai lo shat yan.
佢係老实人

SHORT SENTENCES.

What is this made of?
Ni lik' hai mat ye' tso ke'?

Smell this flower.
Man ha' ni lk fa'.

呢的係乜野做嘅 聞吓呢的花

Do you speak English? Do not let it get wet. What makes him think so?
Ni sek kung fan' wa' mo'? Mok pi kue tsin'g shap. Kue tso mat kom seung?

你識講畨話吆 莫彼佢縶濕 佢做乜咁想

There is no such thing.
Chung mo tse' sz.

Do not touch it.
Mok mo'.

總冇此事． 莫摩

The clock has stopped.
Ni ko shi san' chung 'm hang.

Where did you buy it?
Ni tsoi pin chue mai ke'?

呢個時辰鐘唔行 你在邊處買嘅

I forgot to wind up the clock.
Ngo mong ki seung chung nin.

This watch keeps good time.
Ni ko piu hang tak' ho chun.

我忘記上鐘鍊 呢個錶行得好準

There is no doubt.
'M shai sz yi.

This is very useful.
Ni lik shap fan' yau yung.

唔使思疑． 呢的十分有用

The more the better.
Yuet toh yuet ho.

That is the custom.
Ni lik' hai kwai kue ke'.

愈多愈好． 呢的係規矩嘅

Any body can do it.
Yan yan to' tso' tak'.

Can you swim?
Ni hiu yau shui mo'?

人人都做得． 你曉游水嗎

He is drowned.
Kue chum sz.

Will this do?
Kom yeung tso' tak' mo'?

佢浸死． 咁樣做得嗎

Fill it up.
Fong moon kue.

It must be so.
Pit hai kom.

放滿佢． 必係咁

SHORT SENTENCES.

It can't be so.
Chung 'm hai kom.
總唔係咁．

It must be true.
Si pit tsan' ke'.
是必真嘅

It can't be true.
Pit 'm tak' tsan'.
必唔得真．

Burn it.
Shiu liu kue.
燒了佢

Is that yours?
Ni tik hai' ni ke' mo?
呢的係你嘅嘛.

Don't come again.
'M ho tsoi loi.
唔好再耒

I have a pain in my foot.
Ngo keuk tung.
我腳痛．

Stay here till I come back.
Tsoi ni chue tang' ngo fan' loi.
在呢處等我番耒

How long have you been here?
Ni tsoi ni chue ki kau?
你在呢處幾久

What more do you want?
Ni wan' iu mat ye'?
尔还要乜野

I will come back in a month.
Ngo hue yat ko yuet tsau fan'.
我去一個月就番

I want it done well.
Ngo iu tso ho tik'.
我要做好的

What is this good for?
Ni tik' yau mat yung chue?
呢的有乜用處．

How much do you want?
Ni iu ki toh?
你要幾多

I want some of each kind.
Ngo mooi yeung iu tik'.
我每樣要的．

Have you done with this?
Ni yung yuen mi?
你用完未

This room is too small.
Ni kan fong tai chak.
呢間房太窄．

Lend me one dollar.
Tse' yat ko ngan tsin pi ngo.
借一個銀錢彼我

There is nothing here.
Mo ye' tsoi ni chue.
冇野在呢處．

This is nothing to you.
Ni tik sz yu ni mo kon.
呢的事與你無干

SHORT SENTENCES.

You have made it too wide.
Ni tsò tak' foot kwo tau.
你做得濶過頭.

It is very strange.
Chan hai chut ke'.
真係出奇.

Where does he live?
Kue tsoi pin chue chue`?
佢在边處住.

He cares for nobody.
Kue mat shui too `m pa'.
佢乜誰都唔怕.

Why do you abuse him?
Wai ho ni ma' kue?
為何你罵佢.

I can't bear any more.
Ngo pat nang tsoi yung yan'
我不能再容忍.

When do you begin?
Ni ki shi hoi shau?
你幾時開手.

I want to build a house.
Ngo iu tso yat kan' uk.
我要起一間屋.

The wind blows to-day.
Kom yat ho` tai fong'.
今日好大風.

Have you any business to do?
Ni yau sz tsò mo'?
你有事做嗎.

How many children have you?
Ni yau ki toh tsz nue?
尔有幾多子女

What shall I do?
Tim' yeung ho ni?
點樣好呢

I want to bathe.
Ngo iu sai san'.
我要洗身

He is fit for nothing.
Kue chung mo chung yung.
佢總冇中用

Did you allow him to go?
Ni chun kue hue mo?
你准佢去嗎

I beg your pardon.
Ngo tak' tsooi ni.
我得罪你

Bring me your accounts.
Nim ni tiu sho` loi.
拈呢條數来

That belongs to me.
Ni tik' hai ngo ke'.
呢的係我嘅.

He is busy.
Kue yau sz.
佢有事

Go and buy some fruit.
Hue mai lik kwo tsz.
去買的菓子.

Call him back
Kiu kue hooi loi
呌佢回来

SHORT SENTENCES.

I can not go with you.
Ngo 'm tong ni hue tak.
我唔同你去得

Be careful.
Shiu sum.
小心

Carry it up stairs.
Tam' sheung lau hue.
擔上樓去

It is very well carved.
Ni tik' tiu tak' shum ho.
呢的雕得甚好

He is very civil.
Kue chan ho lai yi.
佢真好禮儀

Clean the table.
Moot kon tsing' ni cheung toi.
抹乾浄呢張枱

You are very clever.
Ni chan tsung ming.
你真聰明

Collect rents.
Shau tso'.
收租

He is compelled to resign.
Kue sai pik ko tooi'.
佢勢迫告退

How shall I compensate you?
Ngo tim' yeung chau tap' ni ho'?
我点樣酬答尔好

He complains to me.
Kue loi ngo shue so uen'.
佢耒我處訴寃

Give him my compliments.
Toi ngo man' hau kue.
代我問候佢

I come to congratulate you.
Ngo tak' loi ho' hi'.
我特耒賀喜

I beg you to consider again.
Ngo tsing' ni tsoi seung kwoh'.
我請尔再想過

You ought to be contented.
Ni ying long chi chuk'.
尔應當知足

Give us a call when convenient.
Yeuk hai tak han' tsing kwo loi.
若係得閒請過耒

Copy this letter.
Chau kwo ni fung shue.
抄過呢封書

Do you know how to count?
Ni shik sz mo.
你識数麼

I see no danger.
Ngo kin' mo ngai im!
我見無危險

It is all delivered.
Yat chung foo kau tsing tso.
一総付交清楚

You may depend upon me.	Ni ho' i lai ngo.	尔可倚賴我
He deserves a reward.	Ying koi ta' sheung kue.	應該打賞佢
What is the difference?	Yau ho fan pit?	有何分別
It is my duty.	Hai ngo poon' fan lik sz.	係我本分的事
You must excuse me.	Ni pit iu kin leung ngo.	尔必要見諒我
I expect him to-day.	Ngo mong kue kom yat to'.	我望佢今日到
Please explain to him.	Ching ni kai ming' kue chi.	請你解明佢知
He has failed in business.	Kue shang i'to' liu poon.	佢生意倒了盆
You do me a favor.	Ni pi ko yan tsing kwoh ngo.	你俾個人情過我
You must find him.	Ni mo sue cham' cheuk kue.	尔務須尋着佢
Give him some thing to eat.	Pi tik ye' kue shik.	俾的野佢食
Help yourself.	Pat yung kue lai.	不用拘禮
I hope he will come.	Ngo mong kue loi.	我望佢未
Did you hurt yourself?	Ni yau seung cheuk mo'?	尔有傷着冇
Very good indeed.	Kwo' in ho'.	果然好
Did you understand what he said?	Ni chi to' kue wa' mat ye' 'm ni?	尔知到佢話乜野唔呢
No, I did not; he was too far from me.	Ngo 'm chi kue li tak' huen' a'h.	我唔知佢離得遠呀
He said that you are very clever:	Kue wa' ni sh.p fa'n ling li:	佢話尔十分伶俐
He is a flatterer:	Kue hai poo cheung yan ke' yan:	佢係煲獎人嘅人

SHORT SENTENCES.

Not at all : I know him well.
`M hai : ngo chi' to' tau' kue lok.

唔係. 我知到透佢㗇

I have not known him long enough.
Ngo se'ung sik kue mo noi.

I have never spoken to him.
Ngo chu'ng mi tsang tu'ng kue kung kwoh!

我相識佢無耐. 我總未曾同佢講過

Shall I introduce you to him?
Che'ung loi ngo chi yan ni tun'g kue se'ung hue' ?

將來我指引你同佢相與

Yes, I would like to make his acquaintance.
Hai che'ung loi ngo chong i'tung kue seung hue.

係. 將來我中意同佢相與

When will you leave this city, sir?
Ni ki shi li ni yat ko fau ni sin shang ?

尔幾時離呢一個埠呢先生

I am going away next week.
Ngo tai yi ko lai' pai' hai' hue loh.

我第二個禮拜係去咯

I shall leave to-morrow morning.
Ngo cheung loi ming chiu tso li hue lok.

我將來明朝早離去咯

How long will you be absent?
Ni tsoi ko chue ki noi ni?

I will be absent two years.
Ngo tsoi ko chue leung nin.

尔在佢處幾耐呢 我在佢處兩年

Will you return to this city ?
Ni cheung loi chung' fa'n loi ni ko fau 'm ni ?

尔將來重番來呢個埠唔呢

Yes, I will ; and bring out my family.
Hai. Ngo che'ung loi tai mai ka' kuen loi tim.

係. 我將來帶埋家眷來添

Do you think it will rain to-day?
Ni koo ko'm yat yau hue lok yau mo ni?

尔佑今日有雨落有無呢

Yes sir, I believe it will.   This is a very cold season.
Hai. Ngo tai cheung loi to` yau.*     *Ni yat sz` hai shap fa'n lang.

係我聯将来都有呢一季係十分冷

It looks like rain, does it not?
Tai ho chue lok hus kom` yau mo` ni?

聯好似落雨咁有無呢

Yes, I think it will rain before night.
Ngo tai kom` ma`n ye hau cheung loi to` yau hue lok

我聯今晚夜後将来都有雨落

If it rains to-night I can't go out.
Tong' yeuk kom ma`n lok hue ngo`m nang' chut hue.

倘若今晚落雨我唔能出去

Will you give this to Ah Chew?
Ni cheung loi pi ni tik kwo` Ah Chew?

尔将来彼呢的過亞釗

When you go home this afternoon?   I will with pleasure.
Ni `ng hau hue kwai ko' shi.   *Ngo si pit ho ni.*

尔午後去歸佢時我是必好呢

Tell him that I thank him very much.
Wa' kwo kue chi ngo shap fun toh che' kue lok.

話過佢知我十分多謝佢咯

I think he is not at home.
Ngo tai kue `m tsoi` ka ha`.

我聯佢唔在家下

He went out this morning at ten o'clock.
Kue hom chiu tso` shap tim chung hue liu lok.

佢今朝早十点鐘去了咯

SHORT SENTENCES.

He said he would not return to-day.
Kue wa' kue kom' yat 'm ooi loi lok.

佢話佢今日唔囬耒咯

Who acts as interpreter when he is gone?
Kue chut hue pin yat ko' tso' chuen wa' ni?

佢出去边一佢做傳話呢

One of the partners can speak English.
Yau ya't ko foh poon' ooi kung hung mo' wa' ke'.

有一佢夥伴噲講紅毛話嘅

I am the interpreter some times.
Ngo yau shi toh' chuen ha' wa'.

我有時都傳吓話

Have you many American customers?
Ni yau ho toh fa' ki hak loi ma'i foh' ah?

尔有好多花旗客耒買貨呀

No sir, we have not many.
'M hai. Ngo ti' mo' ki toh.

唔係．我地毋幾多

Is not your business increasing much?
Ni ti shan'g ii'ho' ho' toh ah?

尔地生意好好多呀

Then come as soon as you can.　Will you wait for me?
Kom ni ho tso' tik loi lok.　*Ni tang' ha' ngo lok?*

咁尔好早的耒嚶．尔莘吓我嚶

I will return in ten minutes.　Very well: Good bye: Good day:
Ngo shap ko mi ni tsau ooi loi lok.　*Ho lok: tsing ha': chi lok:*

我十佢唲力就囬耒咯．好咯．請吓至咯

Call again: I will: Thank you.
Tsoi loi tsau lok: ho lok: ngo si pit.

再耒坐嚶．好咯．我是必

At last he has gone.   I am glad of it.
Tsoi hau` kue hue` liu.   Ngo shap fa'n foon hi`.

在後佢去了． 我十分歡喜

He is very entertaining.   I don't think so.
Kue shap fa'n ho` oon` toi`.   Ngo tai 'm hai.

佢十分好欵待．我睇唔係

I thought he was your friend :
Ngo koo kue hai ni pong yau` :

我估佢係尔朋友

He was once, but he is not now.
Kue yau chue` hai.   Wai hai kom shi 'm hai lok.

佢有次係惟係今時唔係咯

Do you remember that man who came here the other day?
Ni ki tak ko ko yan 'm ni kue ko yat loi ni chue?

尔記得個個人唔呢佢個日耒呢處

Yes sir, I remember him very well.
Hai.   Ngo ki tak kue tsa'n tsa'n lok.

係．我記得佢真真咯

I saw him to-day on the street,
Ngo kom yat tsoi kai` kin kue`,

我今日在街見佢

And he told me he wanted to return to this city again.
Kap kue wa` kwo ngo chi` kue iu` tsoi fa'n loi ni ko fau.

及佢話過我知佢要再返耒呢個埠

Why does he wish to come back?
Wai ho` kue yau se`ung fa'n loi ni?

為何佢又想畨耒呢

I thought he would never return.
Ngo koo kue chun'g mo` fa'n loi lok.

我估佢総無返耒咯

SHORT SENTENCES.

So I thought; but he does not like the country.
Ngo kom̀ koo; wai hai kue 'm chung i tsoi sa'n lue`.

我咁估. 惟係佢唔中意在山裡

How long has he been gone?
Kue hue liu yau ki̇doi lok?

佢去了有幾耐囉

That is no concern of his.
Ngo mo` mat hun sum tung kue kung.

我無乜閒心同佢講

You are very diligent and attentive.
Ni tsan ching` kang lik kaap han sum lok.

你真正勤力及懇心略

As you wish so may you obtain.
U tszè ni kom̀ seung ni shat tso` tak ke`.

如似你咁想你寔做得嘅

What your heart desires may your hand obtain.
Ni ko sum` tsau yuk ni tsau ta:k ke` lok.

你個心就欲你就得嘅咯

There is no sunshine.
Ko chue mo` yat tau chiu ke`.

個處冇日頭照嘅

If you do not believe it is no matter.
Tong ye`uk ni 'm shun` ni to` mo` seung ko`n ke`.

倘若你唔信呢都冇相干嘅

You have a pleasant countenance.
Ni chan ho` hi shik` lok.

你真好氣識略

The currency is not good.
Ko tik choi hi` 'm ho`.

佢的財氣唔好

Get up a little earlier every day.
Chiu chiu hi tso` tik san.

朝朝起早的身

Have you a wife and family?
Ni yau lo` poh yau ka` li mi ni.

你有老婆有家裡未呢

SHORT SENTENCES.

Do not walk disorderly.
Mo ha`ng tak kom` fung chuo`.

無行得咁放次

To-morrow I shall have business.
Ming yat ngo yau tik sz kon.

明日我有的事幹

Now it is very troublesome.
Kom shi chan tsing` fai fan` lok.

今時真正費煩咯

What government officer is this?
Ko ko hai mat wong tai ke` koon ni?

佢個係乜皇帝嘅官呢

He said so day before yesterday.
Kue chin` yat kom` wa`.

佢前日咁話

Every where it is the same.
Kuk chue` kai` tung yat tseu`ng.

各處皆同一樣

What shop has he opened?
Kue hoi mat ye` poo tau ni?

佢開乜野舖頭呢

Much sitting produces illness.
Chi` toh shang pai peng`.

比多生敢病

Speak so that all can understand.
Ko kue` kom` kung ko ko lo` hiu` tak lok.

佢句咁講佢個都曉得咯

He speaks the common dialect.
Kue kung ko tik to` wa` `m ho ke`.

佢講佢的土話唔好嘅

He is really talented.
Ku tsan ho tsoi`ching lok.

佢真好才情咯

By constantly hearing you will understand.
Cheung shi teng` kwan to` hiu tak

常時聽慣都曉得

Don't ask so many questions.
Mok ko`mon kom` toh lok.

莫個問咁多咯

What! read so many books?
Mat ye` wa`! tuk kom` toh po sz lok.

乜野話讀咁多簿書咯

You walk very slowly.
Ni hang tak hom man` ke`.

尔行得咁慢嘅

I bought it myself.
Ngo tsz` ki` mai ke`.

我自己買嘅

SHORT SENTENCES.

What is the number of the house?
Ni kan' fong tai' ki toh ho' ni?

呢間房第幾多號呢

There is a man below.
Ko' chue yau ko' yan tsoi tai'ha'.

Why do you behave so?
Wai ho ni kom'foom lot ni?

佢處有個人在底下，為何你咁欵待呢

He did not conceal any thing.
Kue mi yau sau' mai to' kuk ye'ung ye'.

佢未有修理到各樣野

Why are you here?
Wai ho' ni tsoi ni chue ti ni?

Who sent it to me?
Mat shui ki kwo ngo ke'?

為何你在呢處地呢，也誰寄過我嘅

I can not wait for you.
Ngo 'm tang' tak ni lok'.

How long has he been dead?
Kue sz yau ki noi lok.

我唔等得你咯．佢死有幾耐喽

When shall you go home?
Ni ki shi hue kwai?

In what street do you reside?
Ni tsoi mat ye' kai chue?

你幾時去歸．你在乜野街住

I have friends to dine with me to-day.
Ngo kam yat yau ko pong yau' tung' mai ngo shik' fan.

我今日有個朋友同埋我食飯

How many men live here?
Yau ki toh yan chue' ni chue ni?

What is there worth seeing?
Ko chue tai mat ye' ni?

有幾多人住呢處呢．個處睇乜野呢

Are you going now or not?
Ni kom ha' hue 'm hue ni?

A great many men are wounded.
Sheung liu ho toh yan.

你今下去唔去呢 傷了好多人

I heard some person say so.
Ngo mon yau tik yan kom' wa'.

Have you an answer or not?
Ni yau ooi yum yau mo'?

我聞有的人咁話．你有囘音有冇

SHORT SENTENCES.

He is more skilful than you.
Kue poon sz` che` kwoh`ni

Language should be pure and correct.
Kung wa`.lu ching cho` tsing`.

佢本事似過呢．講話要清楚正

Here there are a great many.
Ni chue ko chue to` ho toh.

呢處佢處都好多

He failed for a very large sum.
Kue sha`t liu yat tiu tai sho`.

At that time it was one o'clock.
Tsoi yat tim` chung ko shi.

佢失了一條大數在一点鐘佢時

I arrived before you.
Ngo to` sin kwoh`ni.

It does not burn readily.
`M hai shap fun ho foh`

我到先過你．唔係十分好火

Return as quick as possible.
Yau kom` fai tak kom` fai fu`n loi lok.

有咁快得咁快返来囉

How do you explain this character?
Ni tim kaai` ni`ko tsze\` ni?

你点解呢佢字呢

A great many men escorted him.
Yau ho toh yan tung kue hue.

有好多人同佢去

I will introduce you to him.
Ngo kue tsin ni hue kue chue hoh.

I am greatly indebted to you.
Ngo tsan tsan im fo` ni lok.

我舉薦你去佢處阿我真真欠員你咯

You speak the dialect of this place.
Ni kung ni chue to` taam.

你講呢處土談

A great many don't understand the dialect.
Ho toh `m hiu ta`k kung ni chue to` wa` ke`.

好多唔曉得講呢處土話嘅

ABOUT INCOME TAX.

Good morning sir.
Tso san sin shang.
How do you do sir?
Ni shap fa'n ho ah'?
Very well, thank you sir.
Shap fa'n ho yau sum`.

早辰先生.你十分好呀.十分好有心

This is my name.
Ni ko hai ngo ming'.
I am tax collector.
Ngo hai sau shui koon.

呢個係我名.我係收稅官

I want you to give me some information.
Ngo seung kiu ni tung` chi ngo.

我想呌尔通知我

Very well; what do you wish to know?
Ho` ni; ni se'ung chi tik mat ye' ni?

好呢.你想知的乜野呢

How much do you make a year?
Ni yat nin chan tak' ki toh ngan ni?

你一年賺得幾多銀呢

I make about $1000 a year.
Ngo tik yat nin chan tak' yat tsin ngan.

我的一年賺得一仟銀

No more?   Is that all?   That's not much.
Mo` lok?    Hai kom toh lok.    Kom` to` m hai ki toh che'.

無囉.係咁多囉.咁都唔係幾多啫

$1000 a year seems a small sum for this store.
Yat tsin ngan ni kan po ho chue siu tik lok.

一仟銀呢間舖好似少的咯

But it is true; I do not make any more.
Hai chan' ke' lok; ngo hai chan' kom' toh che'.

係真嘅囉.我係賺咁多啫

I believe what you say.   I know you tell the truth.
Kom` ngo shun ni suet wa' lok.   Ngo lai ni to kung chan ke'

咁我信你說話咯我聯你都講真嘅

ABOUT INCOME TAX.

Have you paid taxes last year?
Ni kau nin naap ki toh shui ni?

你舊年納幾多稅呢

We did not; we were not yet in business.
Ngo ti kau nin mo naap; ko si 'm tsang hoi cheung tsò shang i.

我地舊年冇納佃時唔曾開張做生意

How long have you been in business?
Ni tsò ki kau shang i lok?

你做幾久生意嘍

It is only about ten months since we started.
Tsin shap ko uet ngo ti chi hi sau tsò che.

前十佃月我地至起首做啫

You sell at wholesale and retail?
Ni tsò seung tau hue kaap san chak tim ah?

你做箱頭與及散拆添唩

We do very little in the retail business.
Ngo ti san mai ho siu che.

我地散賣好少啫

Have you lost money last year?
Ni yau mat kuet ngan yau mo ah?

你有乜決銀有冇唩

We have lost a little from our city customers.
Ngo ti pi poon fau hak tat hue she ngan.

我地彼本埠客撻去些銀

The country customers pay more promptly.
San lue ngan hau in tik.

山裡銀口現的

Do you do much business on credit?
Ni yau ho toh cheung hau ah?

你有好多賬口唩

ABOUT INCOME TAX.

We have to trust all our city customers.
Ngo ti poon fau haak yat chung to hai se' ke' lok.

我地本埠客一總都係賒嘅咯

What is the value of the stock on hand now?
In' shi yau ki to ngan foh chuen ni?

現時有幾多銀貨存呢

It is worth about ten thousand dollars. Have you more than one store?
Yuk' chuen yat maan ngan foh lok. Ni tok yau yat kan po che'?

約存一萬銀貨喱你獨有一間舖啫

We keep three; two in this city and one in the country.
Ngo ti hoi sam kan' poon fau cheuk leung kan san' lue yat kan.

我地開三間本埠着兩間山裡一間

Do you import goods direct from China?
Ni ti tsoi tung san' pan foh loi ah?

你地在唐山辦貨來哇

No sir; we buy nearly all our goods at auction.
'M hai ngo ti yat chung foh to hai tsoi ye' laan mai ke'.

唔係我地一總貨都係在夜冷買嘅

Why don't you import?
Wai hai ni yau 'm tsoi tung san' paan ni?

為係你又唔在唐山辦呢

Because the duty is too high now. How much license do you pay?
Yan wai sui heung chung. Ni naap ki tohngan lai san chi ni?

因為稅餉重你納幾多銀禮臣帋呢

We pay $15.00 per quarter. Have you a license? Let me see it.
Mooi quai ngap ngan shap ng uen. Ni yau naap lai san chi? Pi ngo tai ah.

每季納銀十五元你有納礼臣帋彼我睇下

I can not find it; but it must be in this box.
Ngo 'm chaum tak kin; si pit tsoi ni ko seung chue lok.

我唔尋得見是必在呢個箱處咯

Do you remember having put it in there?
Ni ki tak ko chue lok?

你記得佢處唖

I am sure I placed it in this box.
Ngo tsan tsing ki tak ngo fong ni ko seung chue.

我真正記得我放呢個箱處

Oh! here it is!
Ah! hai chue lok!

Now I have it!
Ngo kin lok!

唖 係處咯 . 我見咯

You live here?
Ni tsoi ni chue chue`?

Is this your store?
Ni kan hai ni po?

你在呢處住 . 呢間係你舖

Are you the owner?
Ni hai sz tau`?

Are you the proprietor?
Ni hai koon li yan?

你係事頭 . 你係管理人

I am the owner.
Ngo hai sz tau`.

The proprietor is not at home.
Koon li yan chut liu kai.

我係事頭 . 管理人出了街

I have no partners.
Ngo mo foh poon.

I keep this store alone.
Ngo chi ki tsò ni kan po che`.

我冇課伴 . 我自己做呢間舖啫

Where are those cigars manufactured?
Ni tik in tsoi pin chue tsò ke` ni?

呢的烟在边處做嘅呢

They are manufactured on Front street.
Ni tik hai tsoi Fat lun kai tsò ke`.

呢的係在佛啥街做嘅

Are they genuine Havanas?
Hai tsing ah won na` lok mi?

係正唖彎拿囉咩

ABOUT INCOME TAX.

No sir; they are only a pretty good imitation.
'M hai; pat kwoh chung tak' ki ho ke' che'.

唔係不過冲得幾好嘅啫

What kind of tobacco do you use?
Ni yung mat ye' in' yip ni?

你用乜野烟葉呢

We use imported tobacco exclusively.
Ngo ti wong si tung chi ki paan in' ke'.

我地往時通自已辦烟嘅

How many men do you employ?
Ni tsing ki toh ko yan ah?

你請幾多個人哑

I am going to the custom-house to pay duty.
Ngo kum hue sui koon kau sui.

我今去税舘交税

I come from the tax collector's office; paid taxes.
Ngo hue sau sui koon chue; kau sui loi.

我去妝税官處交税未

I went yesterday to the internal revenue office.
Ngo 'sok yat hue sau' heung kuk loi.

我昨日去妝餉局未

Do you wish to give security immediately?
Ni seung hue wan taam po yan?

你想去搵擔保人

Yes, if you will accept these two men as bondsmen.
Tung yeuk' ni hang hoi ni' leung ko po ka'.

倘若你肯愛呢兩個保家

He will not accept them if they are not responsible.
Tung yeuk kue 'm hai wan' kue tsau 'm hang ke' lok.

倘若佢唔係穩佢就唔肯嘅咯

VOCABULARY OF USEFUL WORDS.

HOUSE FURNITURE.
Ka' kue sup mat.
家具什物

Barrel. *Pi pa' tung.* 吡吧桶
Basket. *Hong.* 筐
Market basket. *Soong la'm.* 餸籃
Bathing tub. *Sai sun foon.* 洗身盤

Bellows. *Fong se'ung.* 風箱
Bench. *Tiu teng'.* 條櫈
Book-case. *Sue kwai.* 書櫃
Book-stand. *Sue ka'.* 書架
Box. *Seong.* 箱

Letter box. *Sun seung.* 信箱
Broom. *So' kon.* 掃桿
Brush. *Tsat.* 擦
Clothes brush. *Yi fuk tsat.* 衣服擦

Bucket. *Tiu tong.* 吊桶
Bird cage. *Cheuk long.* 雀籠
Oil can. *Yau ping.* 油瓶
Candlestick. *Lap chuk toi.* 蠟燭枱

Cards. *Cho' pai.* 紙牌
Carpet. *Te cheen.* 地氈
Castor. *Ng mi ka'.* 五味架
Case. *Ka'.* 架
Chair. *I'.* 椅

Easy chair. *Hok sz i!* 學士椅
Camp chair. *Ma' chap.* 馬极
Arm chair. *Yau sau i!* 有手椅
Chandelier. *Ye'ung chi teng'.* 洋枝燈

Iron chest. *Tit ka'p ma'n.* 鐵甲萬
Tea chest. *Cha' seung.* 茶箱
Chop stick. *Fy che'.* 快子
Chopper. *Choi io.* 菜刀
Churn. *Ngau yau chung.* 牛油銃

Cleaver. *Chai to'.* 柴刀
Clock. *Si sun chung.* 時辰鐘
Coffee mill. *Ka' fe mo'.* 架啡磨
Cork. *Tsau chat.* 酒櫛
Cork-screw. *Tsau tsuen.* 酒鑽

Couch. *Kau che' chong.* 交子床
Cover. *Koi.* 盖
Cupboard. *Oon tip kwai.* 碗碟櫃
Cradle. *Eu lu'm.* 搖籃
Curtain. *Lim.* 簾

Cushion. *Yi tin.* 椅墊
Decanter. *Pat po li tsau tsun.* 白玻璃酒罇
Writing desk. *Se'tsze' seung.* 寫字箱

VOCABULARY OF USEFUL WORDS.

Dish-cloth.	Tsin poo.	譚布
Dish-cover.	Tip koi.	碟蓋
Duster.	Mo` so`.	毛掃
Fender.	Foh'loo la'n.	火爐欄
Foot-stool.	Keuk tap'tang.	脚踏櫈
Flower-pot.	Fa' poon.	花盤
Frying-pan.	Tit'woo`.	鐵鍋
Grate.	Foh'loo.	火爐
Gridiron.	Tit pa'.	鐵鈀
Kegs.	Pi pa' tung chai.	琵琶桶仔
Kettle.	Cha' po`.	茶煲
Keys.	So' si.	鎖匙
Kindlings.	Chai fa'.	柴花
Jar.	A'ng.	罌
Jug.	Ching.	埕
Ladder.	Tai.	樓
Ladle.	Hok.	殼
Lamp.	Ting'.	燈
Lamp-stand.	Ting toi.	燈枱
Lamp-chimney.	Ting tu'ng.	燈筒
Lamp-shade.	Ting tsau.	燈罩
Lamp-wick.	Ting' sum.	燈心
Lantern.	Ting long.	燈籠
Lock.	So`.	鎖
Mats, or matting.	Tse'k.	蓆
Mill.	Mo'.	磨
Mop.	Poo mak.	布拂
Mortar.	Chung hom.	舂砍
Napkin.	Cha' poo.	茶布
Padlock.	Hop lo' so`.	盒籮鎖
Pail.	Shui tau.	水斗
Water-cask.	Shui tung.	水桶
Pan.	Wo'k.	鑊
Pepper-box.	Hoo tsiu tsun.	胡椒罇
Pestle.	Chung chue'	舂杵
Piano.	Pat yam kom.	八音琴
Picture.	Wa'.	畫
Picture-frame.	Wa' ka'.	畫架
Pipe.	Yin tung.	烟筒
Pipe-stem.	Yin tau.	烟斗
Pitcher.	Tiu kong.	銚缸
Portfolio.	Sz ka'p.	書夾
Rug.	Lo hau chin.	爐口氈
Safe.	Fung ting.	風燈
Scissors.	Kau tsin.	較剪

VOCABULARY OF USEFUL WORDS.

English	Chinese	Romanization
Screen.	屏風	Ping fung.
Folding-screen.	圍屏	Wai ping.
Server.	托盤	Tok poon.
Shears.	大鉸剪	Tai kau chin.
Shelf.	櫃架	Kwai ka.
Shovel.	鏟	Cha'n.
Spade.	剷	Tsan.
Skimmer.	鐵漏殼	Tit lau hok.
Sieve.	篩	Sai.
Snuffer.	燭剪	Chuk tsin.
Sofa.	睡椅	Sui yi.
Sideboard.	條枱	Tiu toi.
Stool.	斗坐	Tau tso'.
Table.	枱	Toi.
Dining-table.	大餐枱	Tai chahn toi.
Round-table.	圓枱	Huen toi.
Square-table.	八仙枱	Pat sin' toi.
Oblong-table.	六仙枱	Lok sin toi.
Card-table.	紙牌枱	Che' pai toi.
Table-cloth.	枱布	Toi poo.
Tea-tray.	茶盤	Cha' poon.
Tea-canister.	茶葉鐏	Cha' ip chun.
Telescope.	千里鏡	Tsin li kin.
Tongs.	鐵鉗	Tit kim.
Trap.	鼠笶	Snue ka'p.
Trunk.	衣槓	Yi lung.
Tub.	盤	Poon.
Flower-vase.	花瓶	Fa' ping'.
Whetstone.	磨刀石	Mo' lo` seak.

CROCKERY—PORCELAIN. Tsi hi. 磁器

EARTHEN-WARE. Nga hi. 瓦器

English	Chinese	Romanization
Bowl.	碗	Oon.
Soup-bowl.	湯碗	Tong oon.
Cup.	杯	Pooi.
Butter-cup.	牛油杯	Ngau yau pooi.
Custard-cup.	吉士杯	Kut si pooi.
Coffee-pot.	架啡壺	Ka' fe ho.
Dish.	碟	Tip.
Gravy-dish.	汁盅	Chup chong.
Silver-plate.	銀碟	Ngan tip.
Large plate.	大碟	Tai tip.
Small plate.	碟仔	Tip tsai.'
Egg-cup.	畳杯	Ta'n pooi.
Platter.	冚兜	Kam tau.

VOCABULARY OF USEFUL WORDS. 75

Tea-cup.	Tea-pot.	Saucer.	Soup-tureen.	Wine-cup.
Cha' pooi.	Cha' hoo.	Cha' tip.	Tung tau.	Tsau pooi.
茶杯	茶壺	茶碟	湯兜	酒杯

GLASS-WARE.		Bottle.		Champagne-glass.
Po li hi.		Po' li tsun.		Sa'm pin pooi.
玻璃器		玻璃樽		三鞭杯

Claret-glass.		Tumbler.		Wine-glass.
Hung tsau pooi.		Shui pooi.		Tsau pooi.
紅酒杯		水杯		酒杯

CUTLERY.	Fork.	Carving-fork.	Table-fork.
To' cha' hi.	Chu'.	Fan cha'.	Tai chan cha'.
刀叉器	叉	分叉	大餐叉

Knife.	Carving-knife.	Table-knife.	Dessert-knife.
To'.	Fan to'.	Tai chan to'.	Kwo' to'.
刀	分刀	大餐刀	菓刀

Butter-knife.		Fish-knife.		Spoon.
Ngau yau to'.		U to'.		Kang.'
牛油刀		魚刀		羹

Gravy-spoon.		Table-spoon.		Sugar-spoon.
Tai kang.'		Tui chan kang.'		Tong kang.'
大羹		大餐羹		糖羹

Tea-spoon.	Soup-ladle.	Cruet-stand.	Coffee-strainer.
Cha' kang.	Tong hok.	Ng mi ka'.	Ka' fe' lau.
茶羹	湯壳	五味架	喫啡漏

DRESS.	Apron.	Bathing-dress.	Bonnet.	Bandbox.
I' fuk.	Wai kwan.	Sai san' sam'.	Nue yan mo'.	Mo' hop.
衣服	圍裙	洗身衫	女人帽	帽盒

Band.	Head-band.	Waist-band.	boots.	Leather boots.
Cheung tai'.	Pau tau.	Foo' tau tai.	Hue.	Pi hue.
長帶	包頭	褲頭帶	靴	皮靴

VOCABULARY OF USEFUL WORDS.

Satin boots.	Water boots.	Breeches.	Braces.	Buckles.
Tuen hue.	Shui hue.	Ngau tau foo.	Foo tai.	Tai kau.
緞靴	水靴	牛頭褲	褲帶	帶扣
Button.	Button-hole.	Canopy.	Cap.	Clasps.
Nau.	Nau moon.	Lo` shan.	Mo` tsai.	Tai kau.
鈕	鈕門	羅傘	帽仔	帶扣
Cloak.	Clogs.	Coat.	Collar.	Clothes—Clothing.
Tui lau.	Muk li.	Tai sam'.	Fong ling.	i fuk.
大褸	木履	大衫	風領	衣服
Corset.	Cravat.	Crown.	Cuff.	Drawers.
Moon hong.	King tai.	Min.	Tsau hau.	Cheung foo.
捫胸	頸帶	冕	袖口	長褲
Flannel drawers.	Cotton drawers.		Dresses.	Fan.
Fa lan` yan foo.	Min poo foo.		i sheung.	Shin.
化蘭仁褲	棉布褲		衣裳	扇
Feather fan.	Ivory fan.	Leaf fan.	Paper fan.	Fan case.
Mo` shin`.	Nga shin.	Quai shin`.	Chi shin`.	Shin` cha.
毛扇	牙扇	葵扇	紙扇	扇揸
Fan box.	Fob.	Fur jacket.	Fur long gown.	Gaiters.
Shin` hop.	Piu` toi.	Pi nap.	Pi cheung po`.	Keuk mang.
扇盒	標袋	皮衲	皮長袍	腳喡
Garter.	Girdle.	Leather girdle.	Gloves.	Handkerchief.
Maat tai.	Tai`.	Pi tai`.	Shau` lup.	Shau` kan.
襪帶	帶	皮帶	手笠	手巾
Grass cloth handkerchief.		Silk hankkerchief.		Hat.
Ha` po kan.		Si kan'.		Mo`.
夏布巾		絲巾		帽
Felt hat.	Summer hat.	Straw hat.	Winter hat.	Jacket.
Chin` mo`.	Leung mo`.	Tso` mo`.	Nuen mo`.	Saam`.
氊帽	涼帽	草帽	暖帽	衫

VOCABULARY OF USEFUL WORDS. 77

Knee pads.	Lappet.	Leggins.		Neck-cloth, or neckerchief.
Pau' sat.	Saam' kam.	Hoo.		Keng' kan.
包膝.	衫襟.	褲.		頸巾

Pantaloons.	Petticoat.	Pocket.	Cue strings.	Robe.
Foo.	Kwun.	Toi'.	Pin sin'.	Po.
褲.	裙.	袋.	辮線.	袍

Ribbons, or tape.	Sandals.	Cord sandals.	Crape sash.
Fai' tsai.'	Chin li ma'.	Tso' hai.	Chau sa' tai.
帶仔.	千里馬.	草鞋.	縐紗帶

Shawl.	Embroidered shawl.	Shirt.	Shoes.	Wooden shoes.
Taap pok' kan.	Sau fa' taap pok' kan.	Hon sam'.	Hai.	Muk hai.
搭膊巾	繡花搭膊巾	汗衫.	鞋.	木鞋

Lady's shoes.	Shoe strings.	Socks.	Woolen stockings.	Silk stockings.
Nue yan hai.	Hai tai'.	Mat tau.	Chin mat'.	Si mat'.
女人鞋.	鞋帶.	襪頭.	氈襪.	絲襪

Stomacher.	Surplise.	Suspenders.	Tassel.	Cotton trowsers.
Nuen too.	Ka' sa'.	Shap tsz tsai.	Mo' soi.	Min foo.
煖肚.	袈裟.	十字帶.	帽繸.	棉褲

Silk trowsers.	Turban.	Veils.	Vest, or waistcoat.	Purse.
Chau foo.	Tau pa'.	Cheung min sa'.	Pooi sum.	Ho pau.
綢褲.	頭帕.	障面紗.	背心.	荷包

One pair of shoes.	One pair of stockings.	Sleeping gown.
Yat tooi hai.	Yat tooi mat'.	Shui po'.
一對鞋.	一對襪.	睡袍

One suit of clothes.	One pair of trowsers.
Yat toi i'fuk.	Yat tiu foo.
一套衣服.	一條褲

BEDROOM.	Bed.	Bedding.	Bed-cover.	Bed-curtain.
Shui fong.	Chong.	Chong poo.	Pi min.	Mun cheung
睡房.	床.	床鋪.	被面.	蚊帳

VOCABULARY OF USEFUL WORDS.

Mattress.	Sheet.	Coverlet.	Bolster.	Pillow.
Yuk tsai.	Pi' taan.	Fu' pi min.	Cheung chum' tau.	Chum' tau.
褥仔.	被單.	花被面.	長枕頭.	枕頭.

Pillow-case.	Blanket.	Clothes-basket.	Cradle.
Chum' tau toi.	Chin.	'Ii fuk lop.	Ngo chong.
枕頭袋.	氈.	衣服笠.	擸床.

Curtain.	Musquito whip.		Cotton quilt.
Mun cheung' me.	Mun fat.		Min tooi.
蚊帳眉.	蚊拂.		棉胎.

DRESSING-ROOM.	Armlets.	Anklets.	Court beads.
So chung lau.	Heung pau.	Keuk ak'	Chiu chue.
梳粧樓.	香包.	腳鈪.	朝珠.

Aromatic beads.	Boot-jack.	Bracelets, or bangles.	Silver bangles.
Heung chue.	Tuet hue pan.	Sau ak'.	Nyan sau ak'.
香珠.	脫靴板.	手鈪.	銀手鈪.

Gold bangles.	Jade bangles.	Shaving-brush.	Tooth-brush.
Cum sau ak'.	Yuk-sau ak'.	Soo tsat'.	Nga' tsat.
金手鈪.	玉手鈪.	鬚擦.	牙擦.

Hair-brush.	Cane.	Card-box.	Casket.	Chain.
Fat' tsat'	Pin kon.	Tip hop.	Sau sik seung.	Lin.
髮擦.	鞭杆.	帖盒.	首飾箱.	鍊.

Silver chain.	Gold chain.	Watch chain.	Comb.
Ngan lin.	Cum lin.	Piu lin.	Soh.
銀鍊.	金鍊.	錶鍊.	梳.

Ivory comb.	Tortoise shell comb.	Wooden comb.	Cosmetic.
Nga' soh.	Toi mooi soh.	Muk soh.	Shui fan.
牙梳.	玳瑁梳.	木梳.	水粉.

Dressing-table.	Dressing-case.	Ear-rings.	Silver ear-rings.
So lau toi.	Keng' chong.	Yi wan'.	Ngan yi wan'.
梳頭枱.	鏡粧.	耳鐶.	銀耳鐶.

VOCABULARY OF USEFUL WORDS. 79

Gold ear-ring.	Finger-ring.	Silver ring.	Gold ring.	Hair pin.
Cum yi wan.	Kai chi.	Ngan kai chi.	Cum kai chi.	Chai.
金耳鐶	戒指	銀戒指	金戒指	釵

Silver hair pin.	Looking-glass.	Mirror.	Necklace.	Needle.
Ngan chai.	Chiu min` keng`.	Sau keng`.	Keng` lin.	Chum.
銀釵	照面鏡	手鏡	頭鍊	針

Parasol.	Perfumery.	Pomatum.	Pin.	Breast-pin.
Yeug che' tsai.	Heong mat.	Heong yau.	Tai tau chum.	Sum hau chum.
洋遮仔	香物	香油	大頭針	心口針

Pin-case.	Pin-box.	Pin-cushion.	Razor.	Razor-strop.
Chum tung.	Chum seong.	Chum chin.	Tai` to.	Hot to pi.
針筒	針箱	針氈	剃刀	喝刀皮

Oil of roses.	Rouge.	Scissors.	Shaving-case.	Perfumed soap.
Mooi quai yau.	In chi.	Kau chin.	Tai` soo seung.	Heong kan.
玫桂油	胭脂	鉸剪	剃鬚箱	香覵

Sponge.	Talisman.	Thimble.	Thread.	Cotton thread.
Shui po.	Kuam tau foo.	Chum ting.	Sin.	Ma sin.
水泡	裰頭符	針頂	線	蔴線

Silk thread.	Tooth-pick.	Tooth powder.		Tooth powder box.
Si sin.	Nga' tsim.	Nga' fooi.		Nga fooi hop.
絲線	牙簽	牙灰		牙灰盒

Towel.	Tweezer.	Umbrella.	Bib.	Vandyke.	Wash-stand.
Min` kan.	Nip kim.	Che`.	Hau shui kin.	Wan kin.	Min` poon ka'.
面巾	鑷鉗	遮	口水肩	雲肩	面盤架

QUADRUPEDS.	Antelope.	Ape.	Ass.	Bear.	Boar.
Tsau sau.	Che'ung.	Yuen.	Lo.	Hung.	Chue kung.
獸	麢	猿	驢	熊	猪公

Wild boar.	Buck.	Buffalo.	Bull.	Calf.
Ye' chue.	Mau luk.	Shui ngau.	Ngau koo.	Ngau tsai!
野猪	牡鹿	水牛	牛牯	牛仔

VOCABULARY OF USEFUL WORDS.

Camel	Cat.	Chamois.	Colt.	Cow.	Deer.
Lok tó.	Mau.	Ling yeung.	Maʻ tsai.'	Wong ngau.	Luk.
駱駝	貓	羚羊	馬仔	黃牛	鹿

	Musk deer.			Spotted deer.	
	Sheʻ.			Kam tsin luk.	
	麝			金錢鹿	

Doe.	Dog.	Elephant.	Fawn.		Fox.
Yau.	Kau.	Tseʻung.	Ngai.		Fue li.
麀	狗	象	麑		狐狸

Gelding.	Goat.	Kitten.	Kid.	Leopard.	Lion.
Shin maʻ.	Tso yeung.	Miu tsai.	Yeung tsai.'	Pau.	Sz tsai.'
騸馬	草羊	貓仔	羊仔	豹	獅仔

Horse.	Mare.	Marmot.		Mole.	Monkey.
Maʻ.	Maʻ naʻ.	To' poot shue.		Tin shue.	Maʻ lau.
馬	馬乸	土撥鼠		田鼠	馬騮

Mouse.	Mule.	Orangoutang.			Otter.
Shik shue.	Loi.	Sing sing.			Shui chaʻt.
石鼠	騾	猩猩			水獺

Sea otter.	Ox.	Pig.	Porpoise.		Rabbit.
Hoi chaʻt.	Im ngau.	Chue tsai.	Ho' tuen.		To'.
海獺	閹牛	猪仔	河豚		兔

Rat.	Water rat.	Rhinoceros.	Seal.		Fur seal.
Lo shue.	Kue shue.	Sai ngau.	Hoi kau.		Chi maʻ tiu.
老鼠	渠鼠	犀牛	海狗		芝蔴貂

Sheep.	Sow.	Squirrel.	Stag.		Stallion.
Min yeʻung.	Chue naʻ.	Sung shue.	Mi.		Mau maʻ.
綿羊	猪乸	鬆鼠	麋		牡馬

Tapir.	Tiger.	Unicorn.	Weasel.	Wolf.	Zebra.
Pak pau.	Lo' foo'.	Ki lun.	Yau shue.	Chai long.	Pung ngau.
白豹	老虎	麒麟	鼬鼠	豺狼	幫牛

VERBS.

Abandon.	Abuse.	Accept.	Accommodate.
Tiu hi`.	Li` ma`.	Tsip shau.	Tse` tso.
丟棄	詈罵	接受	借助
Accompany.	Accomplish.	Accumulate.	Acknowledge.
Tung hang.	Tsun kung.	Tsik chuc`.	Ying.
同行	竣工	積貯	招認
Acquit.	Add.	Address.	Advertise.
Shik fong.	Ka tim.	Min kung.	Pin chuen.
釋放	加添	面講	遍傳
Allow.	Announce.	Annoy.	Answer.
Chun tso.	Chuen po`.	Faan iu`.	Taap ying`.
准做	傳報	煩擾	答應
Arrest.	Ask.	Assent.	Assign.
Chuk na`.	Fong mun`.	Wan` hang`.	Chiu pai.
捉拿	訪問	允肯	照派
Associate.	Astonish.	Attend.	Avoid.
Seung kau.	King ki.	Shi fung.	Pi` ki.
相交	驚奇	侍奉	避忌
Bail.	Bake.	Bathe.	Bear.
Yan po`.	Foh` hung.	Sai` sham.	Yung yan.
認保	火烘	洗身	容忍
Beat.	Beckon.	Beg.	Beg pardon.
Tsak ta`.	Chiu shau`.	Hat.	Tak tsoei.
責打	招手	乞	得罪
Begin.	Behave.	Believe.	Bend.
Hoi shau`.	Hang toai.	Sun.	Wat kuk.
開手	行爲	信	彎曲
Blaze.	Bleed.	Blot.	Blow.
Foh` im`.	Fong huet.	To oo.	Chui.
火焰	放血	塗污	吹

VERBS.

Blush.	Boast.	Boil.	Bolt.
Hom sau.	Kwa hau`.	Chue.	Shaan.
含羞	誇口	煲	閂
Break.	Breathe.	Bribe.	Bring.
Ta` laen`.	Chui hi`.	Fooi` lo`.	Nim loi.
打爛	吹氣	賄賂	拈來
Calculate.	Call.	Can.	Carry.
Tooi suen`.	Kiu.	Tso` tak.	Taam.
推算	叫	做得	擔
Catch.	Charge.	Chat.	Cheat.
Chuk.	Fun foo`.	Han tam.	Kung pin`.
捉	吩咐	閒談	哄騙
Chew.	Clap.	Clean.	Cohabit.
Tseuk.	Paak shau`.	Kohn tseng`.	Kau hop.
嚼	拍手	乾净	交合
Collect.	Come.	Command.	Commence.
Tsue` tsap.	Loi.	Ling.	Hoi shau`.
聚集	來	令	開手
Commit (crime.)	Conclude.	Condemn.	Confiscate.
Faan` tsooi.	Ting` i`.	Ting` liu tsooi`.	Chung kung.
犯罪	定意	定了罪	充公
Congratulate.	Consent.	Consult.	Contain.
Hoh` hi`.	Wan` chun.	Chum cheuk.	Chong tsoi`.
賀喜	允准	斟酌	裝載
Continue.	Converse.	Convict.	Copy.
Pat tsit.	Kau taam.	Ting` tsooi	Chau se`.
不絕	交談	定罪	抄寫
Correct.	Correspond.	Count.	Cry.
Koh ching`.	Seung foo`.	Sho`.	Tai huk.
改正	相符	數	啼哭

VERBS.

Cure.	Dance.	Dare.	Deal.
I chi.	Tiu` moo´.	Kom´.	Maai` maai`.
醫治	跳舞	敢	買賣
Deceive.	Delay.	Deliver.	Demand.
Hi pin`.	In chi.	Foo kau`.	Mun` to.
欺騙	延遲	付交	問討
Demolish.	Deny.	Depart.	Depend.
Tsak fai.	Pat ying`.	Li hue´.	I` laai`.
折毀	不認	離去	倚賴
Deposit.	Despair.	Despise.	Detect.
Ki chui`.	Mo mong`.	Hing fut.	Cha´ wok.
寄貯	無望	輕忽	查獲
Die.	Diet.	Dig.	Digest.
Sze´.	Kai hau´.	Kwut.	Siu shik.
死	戒口	掘	消食
Dine.	Discharge.	Discover.	Disguise.
Shik taai` tsaan.	Chi keuk.	Cha chut.	Koi tsong.
食大餐	辭郤	查出	改裝
Dishonor.	Dislike.	Dismiss.	Disobey.
Hohn hing.	Pat chong i.	Tui kue.	Pat tsuen.
看輕	不中意	推拒	不遵
Display.	Do.	Doubt.	Draw.
Fan wa´.	Tso.	Sze i.	Laai.
繁華	做	思疑	拉
Draw (water.)	Draw (out.)	Draw (lots.)	Draw (in.)
Kap shui.	Che´ chut.	Tsap chau.	Suk.
汲水	扯出	執籌	縮
Draw (near.)	Draw (a bow.)	Draw (nails.)	Dream.
Yan kan.	Wan kung.	Pat ting.	Faat mung.
引近	彎弓	扳釘	發夢

VERBS

Dress.	Drink.	Drive.	Drown.
Chuen i.	Yum`.	Pin ma`.	Chum sze`.
穿衣	飲	鞭馬	沉死
Dry.	Earn.	Eat.	Educate.
Kohn.	Chaan tak.	Shik.	Kau` kwan.
乾	聽得	食	教訓
Emigrate.	Engrave.	Enslave.	Escape.
Ko yeung.	Tiu hak.	Wai nue.	Tuet to`.
過洋	雕刻	為奴	脫逃
Estimate.	Examine.	Examine (goods.)	Excite.
Koo ka.	Cha tsat.	Im` foh`.	Ye`.
估價	查察	驗貨	惹
Excuse me.	Exercise.	Explain.	Expose.
Kin` leung`.	Hok tsaap.	Kyaai`.	Pai chut.
見諒	學習	解	擺出
Facilitate.	Fail.	Faint.	Fall.
Tsip king.	Shat.	Pe` kuen.	Tit lok.
捷徑	失	疲倦	跌落
Finish.	Fire (guns.)	Flatter.	Float.
Uen liu.	Fong paau`.	Fung` shung.	Fau shui.
完了	放炮	奉承	浮水
Fly.	Follow.	Forget.	Forgive.
Fi.	Kan tsui.	Mong ki`.	She` tsooi`.
飛	跟隨	忘記	赦罪
Gain.	Gamble.	Gasp.	Gather.
Chaan`.	To` tsin.	Hi` kun.	Shau tsap.
賺	賭錢	氣緊	收集
Gaze.	Get.	Give.	Give up.
Chue ting` ngan.	Tak to`.	Pi`.	Kau chut.
注定眼	得倒	被	交出

VERBS.

Go down.	Go home.	Go in.	Go out.
Luk hue`.	Hue` kwai.	Yup hue`.	Chut hue`.
落去	去歸	入去	出去
Go up stairs.	Go down stairs.	Go on board.	Go ashore.
Sheung` lau.	Luk lau.	Hoi shuen.	Mai kai.
上樓	落樓	開船	埋街
Grow.	Guard.	Guess.	Guide.
Shang.	Po oo`.	Chai tok`.	Yan` to`.
生	保護	猜度	引導
Handle.	Hang up.	Hate.	Have.
Nim long.	Kwa` hi`.	Tsang oo.	Yau`.
拈弄	掛起	憎惡	有
Hear.	Hire.	Hope.	Hunt.
Teng.	Koo.	Mong`.	Ta` lip.
聽	僱	望	打獵
Imitate.	Include.	Increase.	Inform.
Hau fat.	Tsoi` noi`.	Ka tsang.	Chi ooi.
效法	在內	加增	知會
Insult.	Intend.	Investigate.	Invite.
Hi foo`.	I` yuk.	Sum kau`.	Tseng`.
欺負	意欲	審究	請
Join.	Joke.	Judge.	Jump.
Hop maai.	Hi wun.	Shum` poon`.	Tiu`.
合理	戲言	審判	跳
Keep.	Kick.	Kidnap.	Kill.
Lau ha.	Tek.	Kwai` laai`.	Shaat sze`.
留下	踢	拐帶	殺死
Kiss.	Kneel.	Knock.	Know.
Chuet tsui`.	Kwai` ha`.	Kau.	Chi.
啜嘴	跪下	敲	知

VERBS.

Labor.	Laugh.	Learn.	Lease.
Kung foo.	Siu`.	Hok.	Pai.
工夫	笑	學	批
Like.	Listen.	Live.	Look.
Chung i`.	Tsing` teng:.	Chue.	Hohn`.
中意	靜聽	住	看
Maintain.	Make.	Melt.	Mend.
Yeung.	Tso`:.	Yung.	Poo`.
養	做	鎔	補
Name.	Navigate.	Neglect.	Nip.
Ming.	Piu yeung.	Toi man.	Kap.
名	漂洋	怠慢	挾
Notice.	Notify.	Nourish.	Need.
Chi kok:.	Tat chi.	Yeung`.	Iu.
知覺	達知	養	要
Obey.	Object.	Observe.	Offend.
Tsun i`.	Kang tso`.	Chi kok:.	Chung chong`.
遵依	揹阻	知覺	冲撞
Order.	Overhear.	Overlook.	Oversleep.
Fun foo`.	Tau teng`.	Koon li`.	Sui chi liu.
吩咐	偷聽	管理	睡遲了
Pack.	Pain.	Part.	Pass
Shau shap.	Tung`.	Fun` hoi.	King kwoh`.
收拾	痛	分開	經過
Pay taxes.	Pay debts.	Pay wages.	Peel.
Naap leung.	Wan chai.	Chi kung ngan.	Mok pi.
納糧	還債	支工銀	剝皮
Pity.	Place.	Play.	Play cards.
Hok` lin.	Fung.	Hi sha`.	Ta` pai.
可憐	故	戲耍	打牌

VERBS.

Promise. *Ying shing.* 應承	Pronounce. *Tiu yam.* 調音	Propose. *Tat i'.* 達意	Protect. *Oo wai.* 護衛
Quake. *Chan pa'.* 振怕	Quarrel. *P'in tsui.* 辯嘴	Quench fire. *Mit foh'.* 滅火	Quench thirst. *Kaai' hot.* 解渴
Raise. *Koo hi'.* 舉起	Read. *Tuk.* 讀	Reason. *Lun li'.* 論理	Receive. *Shau.* 收
Recognize. *Ying tak.* 認得	Recollect. *Ki cheuk.* 記着	Recover. *Tak wan.* 得還	Refuse. *Pat hang.* 不肯
Reply. *Taap.* 答	Report. *Pun po.* 稟報	Request. *Tsing'.* 請	Rescue. *Kau' tuet.* 救脫
Sacrifice. *Tsai' huen.* 祭獻	Sail. *Shai shuen.* 駛船	Salt. *Lok im.* 落塩	Save. *Kau'.* 救
Say. *Wa'.* 話	Scream. *Kwong oo.* 狂呼	See. *Kin'.* 見	Sell. *Maai'.* 賣
Sing. *Cheung'.* 唱	Sleep. *Shui'.* 睡	Smell. *Mun.* 聞	Smile. *Hom siu'.* 含笑
Smoke. *Shik in.* 食烟	Smuggle. *Tsau' sze.* 走私	Speak. *Kong'.* 講	Speculate. *Mau seung'.* 謀想
Spend. *Fai'.* 費	Split. *Lit hoi.* 裂開	Spoil. *Tso' waai.* 做壞	Spread news. *Chuen sun mon.* 傳新聞

VERBS.

Swear.	Swell.	Swim.	Swindle.
Faat shai`.	Chung` hi`.	Yau shui`.	Kong pin`.
發誓	腫起	游水	誆騙
Take.	Talk.	Taste.	Teach.
Nim.	Kung wa`.	Sheung mi` to`.	Kaau` fan.
拈	講話	嘗味道	教訓
Tell.	Tempt.	Testify.	Thank.
Wa`.	Yau` waak.	Ching chue.	Toh tse`.
話	誘惑	証住	多謝
Think.	Throw.	Tie.	Touch.
Seung`.	Pau.	Pong`.	Moh.
想	抛	綁	摩
Translate.	Travel.	Treat.	Tremble.
Faan yik.	Yau hok.	Fun to`.	Fat chun.
繙譯	遊學	歟侍	發振

金山大埠啤嚹道書

同治六年五月廿四日立

THE END

www.ingramcontent.com/pod-product-compliance
Lightning Source LLC
Chambersburg PA
CBHW020303090426
42735CB00009B/1206